Meeting the
Math Standards
With Favorite
Picture Books

by Bob Krech

SCHOLASTIC
PROFESSIONAL BOOKS

New York • Toronto • London • Auckland • Sydney
Mexico City • New Delhi • Hong Kong • Buenos Aires

To my many wonderful students.

*Thanks to Connie Beadle, Susanne Catalina, Janis Gutchigian, Linda LaVoie,
Carol Willie, and Melanie Yost for allowing me to invade their libraries.
Thanks once again to Andrew and Faith for the artwork and writing help.*

Edited by **Joan Novelli**
Cover design by **James Sarfati**
Cover illustrations by **Rebecca Thornburgh**
Interior design by **Holly Grundon**
Interior illustrations by **Cary Pillo** except page 58 by **Paige Billin-Frye**

ISBN 0-439-31889-0

Contents

About This Book 4
Meeting the Math Standards 5

NUMBER
One Hundred Hungry Ants 6
How Much Is a Million? 8
Gator Pie 10
The Doorbell Rang 12
Reproducible Activity Pages 14-16

OPERATIONS
The Grapes of Math 17
Alexander, Who Used
to Be Rich Last Sunday 19
2 x 2 = BOO! 21
A Remainder of One 23
Reproducible Activity Pages 25-28

PATTERNS AND ALGEBRA
The King's Chessboard 29
Six-Dinner Sid 31
Spaghetti and Meatballs for All! 33
Reproducible Activity Pages 35-37

GEOMETRY AND SPATIAL SENSE
The Greedy Triangle 38
Sir Cumference and the First Round Table . . 40
The Village of Round and Square Houses . . 42
Grandfather Tang's Story 44
Reproducible Activity Page 46

MEASUREMENT
Measuring Penny 47
How Big Is a Foot? 49
America's Champion Swimmer:
Gertrude Ederle 51
Arthur's Pet Business 53
Reproducible Activity Pages 55-58

DATA ANALYSIS AND PROBABILITY
A Three Hat Day 59
The Best Vacation Ever 61
If You Give a Mouse a Cookie 63
Reproducible Activity Pages 65-67

REASONING, PROOF, AND PROBLEM SOLVING
Math Curse 68
The Jelly Bean Contest 70
Counting on Frank 72
Reproducible Activity Pages 74-76

More Books for Making Math Connections . . 77

About This Book

Children love stories. Good books and stories connect to our imagination and experience. They inspire, amuse, provoke, and teach. Wouldn't it be great to get the same effect with math? Well, you can! Teaching math through good literature is an effective and engaging way to make connections and build skills. That's what this book is all about. It's a great collection of motivating math activities connected to 25 favorite children's books—and to the National Council of Teachers of Mathematics (NCTM) Principles and Standards for School Mathematics 2000.

The strength of the stories featured here, other than that they are entertaining in themselves, is that they clearly relate to meaningful mathematics. Some, such as the pun-filled *2 x 2 = BOO!*, have been written with that intent. Others, such as *Arthur's Pet Business*, are books in which an aspect of mathematics is an integral part of the story but not the focus.

Each featured title is a springboard into learning standards-based math concepts for elementary students in grades 2–4. Activities for *The King's Chessboard*, for example, will have students plotting to become millionaires by washing the dishes, and exploring numeric patterns along the way. After reading *Counting on Frank*, your students will use reasoning skills to find out just how many marbles it would actually take to fill your classroom.

For each featured title, you'll find a book summary, as well as an easy-to-read list of primary content standards. This book also includes:

- related math vocabulary to share with students
- suggestions for sharing each story
- step-by-step activities to reinforce key math skills and concepts
- reproducible charts, activities, patterns, and games
- suggestions for connecting to other areas of the curriculum
- additional resources for learning more

Tip

The chart on page 5 lets you easily match each featured children's book and the corresponding activities with the content and process standards they support.

Computer Connection
Web sites

These Web sites are terrific resources for any of the areas of mathematics addressed in this book.

Ask Dr. Math: www.mathform.com/dr.math/

A Plus Math: www.aplusmath.com

PBS Mathline: www.pbs.org/teachersource/math.htm

Meeting the Math Standards

Standards

Children's Book Titles	Number	Operations	Patterns and Algebra	Geometry and Spatial Sense	Measurement	Data Analysis and Probability	Problem Solving	Reasoning and Proof	Communication	Connections	Representation
One Hundred Hungry Ants	●	●	●				●	●	●	●	●
How Much Is a Million?	●	●	●				●	●	●	●	●
Gator Pie	●	●	●				●	●	●	●	●
The Doorbell Rang	●	●	●				●	●	●	●	●
The Grapes of Math	●	●	●				●	●	●	●	●
Alexander, Who Used to be Rich Last Sunday	●	●					●	●	●	●	●
2 x 2 = BOO!	●						●	●	●		●
A Remainder of One	●	●	●				●	●	●	●	●
The King's Chessboard	●	●	●				●	●	●	●	●
Six-Dinner Sid	●	●	●				●	●	●		●
Spaghetti and Meatballs for All!	●	●	●	●			●	●	●	●	●
The Greedy Triangle	●	●	●	●			●	●	●	●	●
Sir Cumference and the First Round Table	●	●	●	●			●	●	●	●	●
The Village of Round and Square Houses	●			●			●	●	●	●	●
Grandfather Tang's Story			●	●			●	●	●	●	●
Measuring Penny	●	●			●		●	●	●	●	●
How Big Is a Foot?	●	●			●		●	●	●	●	●
America's Champion Swimmer: Gertrude Ederle	●	●			●	●	●	●	●	●	●
Arthur's Pet Business	●	●			●		●	●	●	●	●
A Three Hat Day	●	●	●		●	●	●	●	●	●	●
The Best Vacation Ever	●	●			●	●	●	●	●	●	●
If You Give a Mouse a Cookie	●	●	●				●	●	●	●	●
Math Curse	●	●	●				●	●	●	●	●
The Jelly Bean Contest	●	●			●	●	●	●	●	●	●
Counting on Frank	●	●	●		●	●	●	●	●	●	●

One Hundred Hungry Ants

by Elinor J. Pinczes (Houghton Mifflin, 1993)

One hundred hungry ants go marching off single file to a picnic. The littlest ant suggests that they'll get there sooner if they split up into two lines of 50. They rearrange themselves as he suggests and continue. As they go, the littlest ant suggests new and more efficient arrangements, but each time it takes the ants a while to reorganize. Finally they reach the picnic in 10 rows of 10— only to find that there's no food left.

Math Vocabulary

column: a vertical arrangement of items, including numbers
pattern: a sequence of objects, events, or ideas that repeat
row: a horizontal arrangement of items, including numbers

Sharing the Story

Give each child a copy of page 14. Can children guess how many ants are on the page? 100! Divide the class into groups and have each use the ants to create as many arrangements of 100 ants as they can. To show their arrangements, have students cut out the ants, arrange them on paper, glue them in place, and then write a description at the bottom—for example, "Two columns of 50 ants each." Combine arrangements on roll paper, then add details to create a picnic scene—with the ants heading for the food!

NCTM STANDARDS

Number and Operations

Understand numbers, ways of representing numbers, relationships among numbers, and number systems.

☼ Count with understanding and recognize "how many" in sets of objects.

☼ Recognize equivalent representations for the same number and generate them by decomposing and composing numbers.

The Ants Went Marching in Patterns

One Hundred Ants

The number one hundred is an important reference point and an interesting quantity to explore with this interactive bulletin board.

1. Give each student a copy of page 14. Have them count the number of ants on the page. (There are 100.)

2. Explain that students are going to create a pattern puzzle using their ants. Students can use the color and placement of their ants to create their pattern. Urge students to create a pattern that is complex enough to challenge their classmates' thinking.

3. Have students plan their pattern, then color their ant squares accordingly and cut them out. Ask students to arrange their ants on drawing paper, then glue them in place when they are sure about the placement.

4. On a separate sheet of paper, have students use words and numbers to explain their pattern—for example, "My placement pattern is ten rows of ten or 10 x 10; my color pattern is red, blue, purple, red, blue, purple."

5. Invite students to display their patterns on a bulletin board using two staples at the top only. Have them staple their explanation paper under the pattern, so that passersby can try to identify the patterns first, then lift the papers to check their guesses.

Materials

- ant patterns (page 14)
- crayons
- scissors
- glue sticks
- drawing paper
- stapler

Try This Too! Word Connections

The French word *cent* means "hundred." Share with students words that begin with *cent* and explore the meaning of each word. For example, *century* is 100 years while a Roman *centurion* was an officer in charge of 100 men. Can the class find any other *cent* words? Go on to explore other words that have a number prefix—for example, *triangle* and *bicycle*.

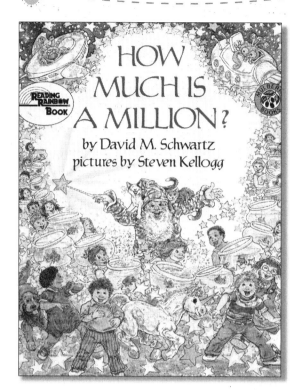

How Much Is a Million?

by David M. Schwartz
(Lothrop, Lee, and Shepard, 1985)

Number and Operations

Understand numbers, ways of representing numbers, relationships among numbers, and number systems.

- Understand the place-value structure of the base-ten system and be able to represent and compare whole numbers and decimals.

- Develop understanding of the relative position and magnitude of whole numbers and of ordinal and cardinal numbers and their connections.

With the guidance of Marvelosissimo, the Mathematical Magician, a group of children and their pets explore just how big a million, a billion, and a trillion are. Exciting, detailed illustrations by Steven Kellogg and the very clear examples take a difficult concept and give children an opportunity to gain some perspective and understanding of these huge numbers.

Math Vocabulary

centimeter (cm): a metric length unit; there are about 3 cm in an inch

rectangle: a quadrilateral with four right angles and opposite sides parallel and the same length

Sharing the Story

Before reading the story, ask students to share the biggest numbers they know. Have them write these on the board, and see if they can name them and give real-life examples that might include quantities as large as these. For example, someone might mention that there could be a thousand ants in a colony or a million grains of salt in a salt shaker. This will help lend context when you share *How Much Is a Million?* and try the followup activities.

My Life in Big Numbers

In *How Much Is a Million?* David Schwartz makes extensive use of multiplication to create larger numbers from the smaller numbers he begins with. Students can apply this same kind of extrapolation while looking at their own lives.

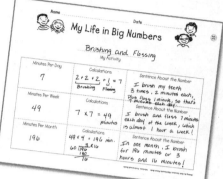

1. As a homework assignment, ask students to choose an activity they do at home and record the number of minutes they do it each day. This might be something simple, such as brushing teeth, or more time-consuming, such as baseball practice.

2. Have students share the homework information with the class. Then ask them to consider how many minutes per week they do the activity. Demonstrate the steps in finding out by calculating how many minutes per week students spend in the cafeteria for lunch. (If students have lunch for 20 minutes a day, they'd multiply 20 times 5 for 100 minutes per school week.)

3. Give everyone a copy of page 15. Ask students to complete the record sheet for their activity, entering the amount of time they do the activity each day, showing the multiplication or repeated addition they used to calculate how much time they spend doing it in a month, year, or even a lifetime, and writing a sentence about the resulting big number. Invite students to illustrate their sheet. Then put the papers together to make a class book of big numbers!

Materials

- record sheet (page 15)
- pencils, crayons, markers
- calculators (optional)

Try This Too! Show Me the Money!

Often when young students think about a million, they immediately think of dollars. Is there a million dollar bill? Is there a thousand dollar bill? Who's on the hundred dollar bill? For answers to these and other intriguing money questions, share *The Ultimate Kids' Money Book* by Neale S. Godfrey (Simon & Schuster, 1998). Divide the class into small groups and assign each a coin or bill. Using this book or other resources, have students research and prepare a short presentation on their assigned piece.

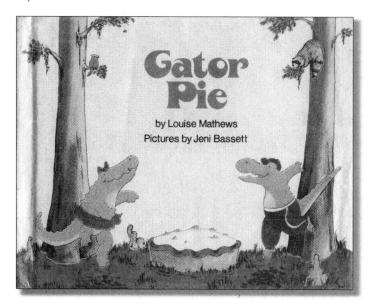

Gator Pie

by Louise Mathews (Dodd, Mead, 1979)

Alvin and Alice, two young alligators, find a pie. They decide to cut it in half and share it, but before they can, another alligator stomps up and demands a piece. More visitors arrive and Alvin and Alice continue to calculate the fractions (pieces) they'll need to cut. When the number of visitors reaches 100, Alice worries that nobody will be happy with the tiny pieces. But Alvin has a plan. He invites the alligators to pick their own piece whereupon a huge fight erupts, allowing Alice and Alvin to slip off with the pie to enjoy on their own. Half for each!

Math Vocabulary

denominator: the number written below the line in a fraction; it tells the number of equal parts in a whole

fraction: a way to describe a part of a whole or a part of a group by telling the number of equal parts in the whole or group and the number of those parts you are describing

numerator: the number written above the line in a fraction; it tells how many equal parts are described by the fraction

Sharing the Story

Before reading *Gator Pie*, have students form groups to set up "fraction museums." Provide each group with plenty of manipulatives, like fraction pieces, attribute blocks, and counting chips, as well as paper, scissors, pencils, and crayons. Ask students to use these materials to create displays showing what they know about fractions. Have them include signs that name the fractions with words and in a number format. Let groups give "guided tours" of their exhibits, explaining the fractions to their visitors.

NCTM STANDARDS

Number and Operations

Understand numbers, ways of representing numbers, relationships among numbers, and number systems.

- Develop understanding of fractions as parts of unit wholes.

- Use models, benchmarks, and equivalent forms to judge the size of fractions.

- Understand and represent commonly used fractions.

One Hundred Pieces of Pie!

Alice faced a tough task when she was trying to cut that pie into hundredths—one hundred equal pieces. It's difficult to cut a pie that way, but students will have fun trying with this activity.

1 Give each student a paper plate "pie." Let students color in the plate to represent a favorite pie. Revisit the story, stopping at the first fraction mentioned. Ask students to mark their plate to represent that fraction. Have them write the fraction that shows what each person will get on the plate. ($\frac{1}{2}$)

2 Give students another paper plate. Continue reading, again stopping when Alice and Alvin tackle a new fraction problem. Have students divide their pie to show the new number of pieces they'll have to cut, and write the resulting fraction that tells how much of the pie each person will get. ($\frac{1}{3}$) Continue, letting students divide more paper plate pies into pieces to represent the various fractions in the story.

3 Continue to explore fractions with a 100-square grid. (See sample, right.) Give each student a copy. Have students color in portions of the grid to model various fractions. For example, to represent $\frac{5}{100}$, they can color in 5 of the 100 squares.

Hundred Chart

1	2	3	4	5	6	7	8	9	10
11	12	13	14	15	16	17	18	19	20
21	22	23	24	25	26	27	28	29	30
31	32	33	34	35	36	37	38	39	40
41	42	43	44	45	46	47	48	49	50
51	52	53	74	55	56	57	58	59	60
61	62	63	74	65	66	67	68	69	70
71	72	73	74	75	76	77	78	79	80
81	82	83	84	85	86	87	88	89	90
91	92	93	94	95	96	97	98	99	100

4 Use the fractions students make to explore decimals. For example, if they color in 15 of the 100 squares, that's $\frac{15}{100}$ which can be written ".15." This translates well to money and the understanding that 15 cents, also written .15, is $\frac{15}{100}$ of a dollar.

Materials

❋ paper plates

❋ crayons, markers, pencils

Tip

For more fun with food and fractions, read *Eating Fractions* by Bruce McMillan (Scholastic, 1991). Let students use some of their fraction knowledge by following the recipes in the back of the book and dividing up the final products—the food!

Try This Too! All About Alligators

How long do alligators live? How long do they grow? Investigate number-based facts about alligators with Jim Arnosky's *All About Alligators* (Scholastic, 1994). Then have students use fractions and their new alligator knowledge to create alligator fraction word problems—for example, "If $\frac{1}{2}$ of an alligator weighs 35 pounds, how much does the whole alligator weigh?"

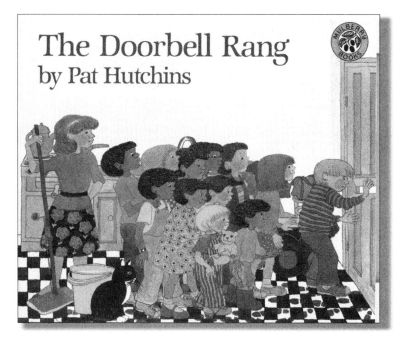

The Doorbell Rang
by Pat Hutchins

The Doorbell Rang

by Pat Hutchins (Greenwillow, 1986)

NCTM STANDARDS

Number and Operations

Understand numbers, ways of representing numbers, relationships among numbers, and number systems.

☀ Count with understanding and recognize "how many" in sets of objects.

Understand meanings of operations and how they relate to one another.

☀ Develop fluency in adding, subtracting, multiplying, and dividing of whole numbers.

Victoria and Sam's mother makes a plate full of cookies for the children to share. In fact there's a dozen just for the two of them, but then the doorbell rings and in come Tom and Hannah to share the cookies as well. The doorbell continues to ring, and more and more neighbors are invited in for cookies. Soon there's only one cookie for each child, then the doorbell rings once more and there's grandma with a huge tray of cookies.

Math Vocabulary

division: the process of separating into two or more parts, areas, or groups

Sharing the Story

After reading and discussing the story, reread it, this time asking students to use the chart on page 16 to keep track of what's going on with the cookies. As new characters enter the story ask students to record the number of cookies, the number of children, and the number of cookies each child would get. At the end of the story, have students examine their numbers. What sorts of relationships do they see? What if two more children came? and then two more?

Fair Shares

In this story, there was an even number of cookies, and children were arriving by twos so that it was possible to share the cookies evenly. Use this activity to explore what might happen if things were not so simple.

Materials

* construction paper
* scissors
* cookies (optional)

1. Pose the following problem: "Victoria and Sam's mother made 12 cookies. Three friends showed up at the door. Mom told them to share fair. How could they divide the cookies?"

2. Have students work with a partner to solve the problem. Ask students to cut out a dozen construction-paper cookies and use them to share their solution with the class.

3. Use this activity and students' solutions as an example of real-life division and remainders. Let students take turns at the chalkboard writing a division sentence that corresponds to their solution.

4. For a truly real-life application of the math in *The Doorbell Rang*, share a box of cookies with the class. Before enjoying the treat, count the cookies and ask students to show how they can share the cookies fairly. (Check for food allergies before students eat the cookies.)

Try This Too! Cooking Up Some Math

Lots of cookies were baked in *The Doorbell Rang*. For some fun exploration into cooking, take a look at favorite cookie recipes. Let pairs of students select a recipe. Ask students to decide how many cookies each person in the class would get if they made the recipe. What if they doubled it? Tripled it? Encourage students to write division sentences that show their solutions. Consider mixing up a batch and then doing the division for real.

One Hundred Ants

Meeting the Math Standards With Favorite Picture Books   Scholastic Professional Books

My Life in Big Numbers

My Activity _____

Minutes Per Day	Calculations	Sentence About the Number
Minutes Per Week	Calculations	Sentence About the Number
Minutes Per Month	Calculations	Sentence About the Number

Name _____ Date _____

The Doorbell Rang

Number of Cookies	Number of Children	Number of Cookies Each Child Should Get

Meeting the Math Standards With Favorite Picture Books   Scholastic Professional Books

The Grapes of Math

by Greg Tang (Scholastic Press, 2001)

Clever rhymes matched with colorful illustrations of groups of objects like bees, fish, cherries, and camels make for an interesting excursion into poetry and math. Each rhyme describes a set of objects in a picture and a way to count them. The reader must use the clues in the rhyme to figure out the number of items. The counting strategies hinted at in the clues include a variety of operations and problem-solving strategies and are described in detail in an index at the back of the book.

Math Vocabulary

strategy: a careful plan or method

Sharing the Story

One of the best ways to use *The Grapes of Math* is to concentrate on one rhyme at a time. Read one page and let students think about, discuss, and explore the picture rather than read the book straight through. Ask students if they can figure out a way to find out how many objects are on the page without counting one by one. Have them generate possible strategies for finding the correct number.

NCTM STANDARDS

Number and Operations

Understand numbers, ways of representing numbers, relationships among numbers, and number systems.

- Recognize "how many" in sets of objects.

- Recognize equivalent representations for the same number.

Understand meanings of operations and how they relate to one another.

- Understand addition and subtraction of whole numbers and the relationship between the two operations.

number Garden

Materials

☀ flower patterns
   (page 25)

☀ crayons, markers

☀ scissors

☀ pushpins

Continue to explore counting strategies through addition and subtraction with an activity that lets your students try their hand at arranging flowers.

1. Set up a bulletin board display in the hall, covering the background with a solid color.

2. Give each student a copy of page 25. Have children color and cut out the flowers. Divide the class into small groups. Have children in each group combine their flowers, and experiment with different ways to arrange them. Encourage children to consider arrangements that lend themselves to a counting/addition strategy for finding the total number.

3. Let each group place their flowers on the bulletin board as desired, using pushpins to tack them up. Ask students in each group to write a rhyme or series of clues to go with their arrangement, as Greg Tang did in *The Grapes of Math*, and place it next to their flowers.

4. Have each group create an answer key that includes an explanation of the intended strategy. Then have them place it next to the corresponding arrangement under a flap of paper labeled "Answer."

5. To go further, select one page and read it aloud. Have students work with a partner to record an addition sentence that describes one way to determine the number of objects in the picture. For example, if Tang suggests noticing that there are 4 groups of 4 in a picture (a 4 x 4 square), and then 5 more objects outside, students might write 4 + 4 + 4 + 4 = 16 and 16 + 5 = 21, or 4 + 4 + 4 + 4 + 5 = 21.

Three rows of three
That's what I see
Now add two
That's all, You're through!

Lift For Answer

Try This Too! Counting Quickly Contest

Let students compare one-by-one counting with a counting strategy such as counting by fives (or any of the other strategies highlighted in *The Grapes of Math*) with this activity. Draw two identical sets of dots on the chalkboard. Now challenge a student to a counting race. You count by ones and let the student use a strategy. Who finishes first? Who is most accurate? Help students recognize that an efficient strategy is fast and accurate.

Alexander, Who Used to Be Rich Last Sunday

by Judith Viorst (Macmillan, 1978)

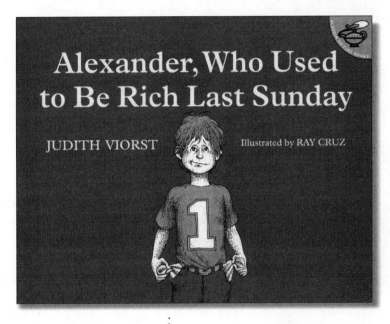

Alexander's brother Anthony has money. His brother Nicholas has money. All Alexander has is bus tokens. Alexander remembers back to last Sunday when he got a dollar from his grandparents. As the day progressed, the dollar slowly disappeared—he made purchases, lost bets, rented a snake, and engaged in a variety of other costly endeavors.

Math Vocabulary

regroup: to form into a new grouping in order to add or subtract

subtraction: the operation of deducting one number from another

Sharing the Story

After reading *Alexander, Who Used to Be Rich Last Sunday*, have students recall the ways Alexander spent or lost money. Ask: "Did he really spend his whole dollar?" Suggest reviewing the story in an organized way to find out for sure. Have students write $1.00 at the top of a sheet of paper. Reread the story aloud, stopping at each page where money is spent or lost to let students record the subtraction problem that occurs. At the end of the book, check to see what the final result is. Is all of the dollar really gone?

NCTM STANDARDS

Number and Operations

Understand meaning of operations and how they relate to one another.

☀ Understand the effects of adding and subtracting whole numbers.

Compute fluently and make reasonable estimates.

☀ Develop and use strategies for whole-number computations.

_____, Who Used to Be Rich Last Sunday

After reading the story and seeing the pattern of Alexander's spending, have students try this blend of story writing, art, and math.

1. After sharing the story, discuss how Alexander spent his money. Encourage children to notice patterns in his spending.

2. Give each child a copy of page 26. Explain that students will be filling in word balloons and adding illustrations to tell their own "Alexander" stories— substituting themselves as the main character.

3. Decide on the starting amount of money based on students' readiness. Explain that the objective is to finish with a total of zero—just like Alexander. Students can keep a running tally in the boxes provided to help with accuracy.

Try This Too! Dollar-Bill Relay Race

This fun relay race involves counting bills of different denominations. Place three chairs at one end of the room and set a hat on each. Place a tape line in front of the chairs. Have students line up in three teams behind a tape line at the other end of the room. Place a stack of play money (different denominations) on the tape line in front of each team. Start some music and have the first student on each team place a bill from the stack on his or her head. (You might provide each child with an inexpensive hairpin to hold the bill in place.) Have students walk to the other end of the room, take the bill off their heads when they cross the second tape line, and place it in the hat. Have them walk quickly back to their team and tag the next person, who repeats the procedure. This continues until you stop the music. At that time, have team members calculate the value of the bills in their hat. The team with the highest total amount of money is the winner.

2 x 2 = BOO!
A Set of Spooky Multiplication Stories

by Loreen Leedy (Holiday House, 1995)

Witches, cats, bats, skeletons, mad scientists, and other spooky creatures get involved in situations that use multiplication from zero to five in this colorful, cartoon-filled picture book. There are plenty of puns and gruesome goings-on to get children chuckling and thinking about multiplication.

Math Vocabulary

array: an arrangement of objects in equal rows
fluency: the quality of being effortlessly smooth, rapid
multiplication: the operation of repeated addition of the same number

Sharing the Story

Before reading *2 x 2 = BOO!*, have students share their Halloween stories. Ask questions about costumes they wore, decorations they enjoyed, and favorite treats. Use the stories as a basis for formulating some multiplication problems on the chalkboard—for example, "Five people say they each got 10 popcorn balls. How many popcorn balls would that be?" Tell students that in the story they are about to hear, there will be many similar multiplication examples.

NCTM STANDARDS

Number and Operations

Understand meanings of operations and how they relate to one another.

☀ Understand various meanings of multiplication and division.

☀ Understand the effects of multiplying and dividing whole numbers.

Compute fluently and make reasonable estimates.

☀ Develop fluency with basic number combinations for multiplication and division.

Bat Cave Bulletin Board

Materials

- ☼ bat patterns (page 27)
- ☼ construction paper
- ☼ pencils
- ☼ scissors
- ☼ laminating machine (optional)
- ☼ Velcro strips
- ☼ glue or tacks

Tip

Bats are fascinating creatures. Read *Bats: Mysterious Flyers of the Night* by Dee Stuart (Carolrhoda, 1994). Then invite students to add science facts about bats to the bulletin board caves.

Students work their way across this bulletin board to master bat caves full of math facts!

1. Make enough copies of page 27 so there is one bat for each student.

2. Begin by focusing on two sets of multiplication facts. On a bulletin board, make simple construction paper caves—one for each set of facts you want to practice. So, you might have a "twos cave," a "threes cave," and so on.

3. Assign individual facts from the sets to students. Have them write the factors on the front of their bat and the product on the back. Laminate the bats, if desired, and have students cut them out.

4. Glue 10 Velcro strips on each cave and one strip to the back of each bat. (You could also use tacks.)

5. Have students take turns sharing their facts and placing their bats in the correct cave. Let students continue to explore the bat caves by trying to answer all the facts in a cave. They can remove the bats to check their answers on the back. Students can also borrow the bats from the caves for fact practice games—and easily return them when they're finished.

Try This Too! Bat Arrays

Arrays are an excellent way for students to gain an understanding of multiplication and experience facts on a pictorial level. Make multiple copies of the bat patterns on page 27. Cut out the bats and place them at a center. Let students visit the center and arrange the bats to match a series of facts—for example, twos. Looking at arrays in this way can also show students how "turn around" facts (2 x 4 = 4 x 2) work.

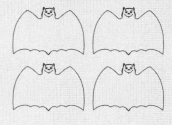

A Remainder of One

by Elinor J. Pinczes (Houghton Mifflin, 1995)

The Twenty-Fifth Insect Squadron marches in parade formation. Each bug has a partner, except Soldier Joe. The Queen is not happy to see Soldier Joe alone. She likes things tidy and organized, and orders Joe to leave the parade. Joe stays up all night trying to think of a solution. The next day the ants march again, this time in groups of three. Joe again is left out and ordered home. The next day four lines of six march and Joe again is left out. When the 25 soldiers finally form lines of five, Joe is included.

Math Vocabulary

remainder: in whole number division, when you have divided as far as you can without going into decimals, what has not been divided yet is called the remainder.

Sharing the Story

After reading the story, let students take turns showing the math for the parade formations that made Joe a "remainder." Have students write a short math story of their own that describes a situation, preferably from real life, in which there would be a remainder. Have students also write a division sentence that matches the story. Use students' stories as a source of word problems for the class to solve.

NCTM STANDARDS

Number and Operations

Understand meanings of operations and how they relate to one another.

☼ Understand various meanings of multiplication and division.

☼ Understand the effects of multiplying and dividing whole numbers.

Compute fluently and make reasonable estimates.

☼ Develop fluency with basic number combinations for multiplication and division.

Insect Parade

Students make their own insect parades to further explore division and remainders.

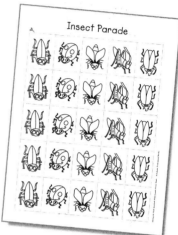

1. Give each student a copy of page 28, which has 25 insects, just like in Joe's Army. Have students color and cut out their insects.

2. Review some of the parade formations in the story. Let students experiment with arranging their insects in those and other formations. Have them glue their insects on construction paper in the formation of their choice.

3. Ask students to write a division sentence describing their formation. For example, if they divide the 25 insects into two rows of 12 with a remainder of one, they would write $25 \div 2 = 12$ R1.

4. Invite students to share their formations and division sentences. Compare them with the formations in the book. Were all the arrangements from the book represented in students' work? How many formations are possible without cutting insects in half? (Joe would not like that strategy!)

Materials

- insect patterns (page 28)
- scissors
- crayons, markers
- construction paper
- glue

Try This Too! Flip Facts

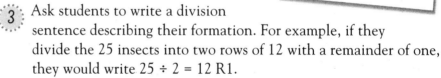

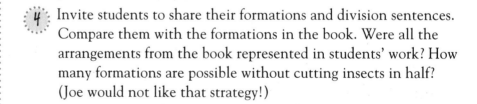

These fun flash cards help students learn facts while using multiplication as a strategy for solving and checking division. To make the flash cards, write division facts on index cards—for example, $20 \div 5 =$ (one fact per card). Give each student a card. Have students write the related multiplication fact on the other side. So, for $20 \div 5 =$ the student would write $4 \times 5 = 20$. Collect the cards and let students use them to quiz each other. (Or use them with the class when you have a few spare minutes and want to practice math facts.) Have students read the division fact, answer the problem, and give the multiplication problem that would prove and check the answer.

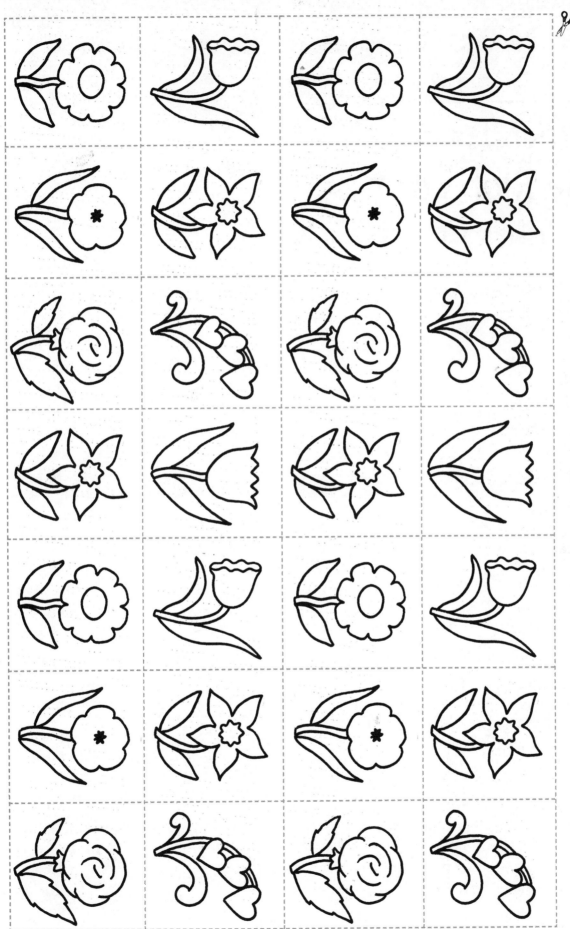

Number Garden

_____,

Who Used to Be Rich Last Sunday

Tally

Tally

Tally

Tally

Tally

Bat Facts

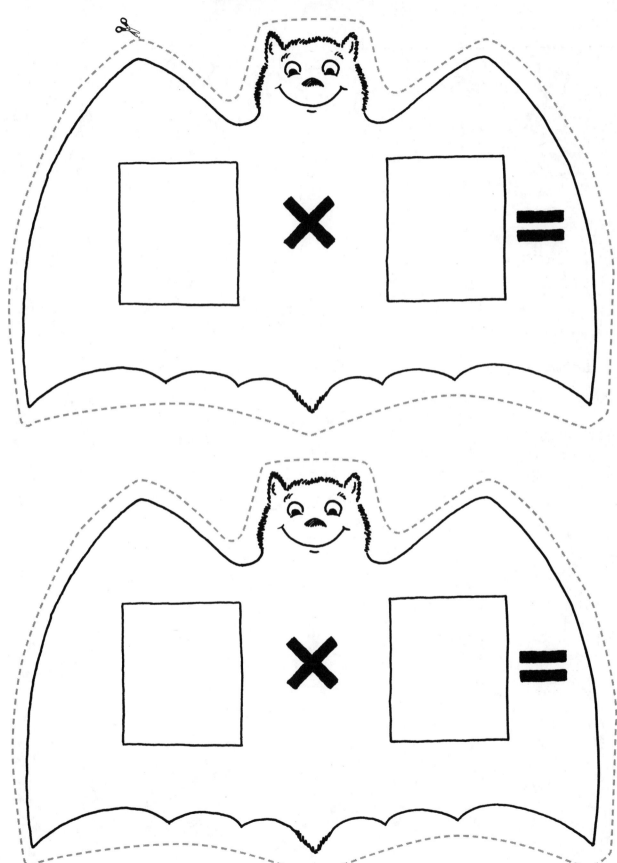

27

Insect Parade

Meeting the Math Standards With Favorite Picture Books   Scholastic Professional Books

The King's Chessboard

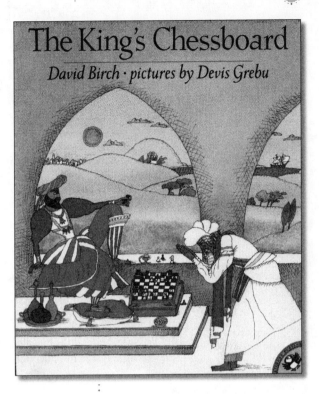

The King's Chessboard
David Birch · pictures by Devis Grebu

by David Birch (Penguin Puffin, 1988)

In ancient India, a wise man has faithfully served his king for many years. The king wants to reward him, but the wise man graciously declines. The king, however, insists and finally forces the wise man to accept a reward. The wise man assents and tells the king, "I only ask this: Tomorrow, for the first square of your chessboard, give me one grain of rice; the next day, for the second square, two grains of rice . . . and so on for every square of the chessboard." The king agrees, but it soon becomes apparent that before long there will not be enough rice in all the kingdom or even in all the world to pay the wise man. The king learns more than just a mathematical lesson from the wise man's request.

Math Vocabulary

algebra: a branch of mathematics that uses variables to express rules about numbers, number relationships, and operations

Sharing the Story

The king's chessboard is a key element in this story. Before reading, ask your class how many students play chess. Bring in a chessboard and pieces and ask students what kinds of math, particularly problem solving, they see in the game. Ask them what other games involve math and strategy. Children may be surprised to see that the math they've been doing at school is the same math they've been using in the games they've played for years.

NCTM STANDARDS

Algebra
Understand patterns, relations, and functions.

❋ Analyze how repeating and growing patterns are generated.

❋ Describe, extend, and make generalizations about geometric and numeric patterns.

Well-Paid

Materials

- paper
- pencils
- calculators
- graph paper
- pennies

In *The King's Chessboard*, the concept of doubling creates some very large numbers very quickly. This doubling pattern can be even more exciting when applied to money!

1. A common household chore for children is washing dishes. Provide students with a set of materials, and ask them to work out how much money they would be paid if they earned one cent for the first day of washing dishes, two cents for the second day, four cents for the third day, and so on, using the same doubling pattern for a month (30 days).

2. Once students have grappled with this for a while, provide calculators and show how to double numbers by entering "2 x" followed by "=." Once the calculator is preset in this manner, enter a number, then press "=" and it will automatically double the number.

3. Let students use their preset calculators to determine their earnings, starting by entering ".01" and then pushing "=" 29 more times to watch the money grow. It will be well worth it! (It seems impossible, but on day 30 the dishwasher would be paid $5,368,709.20. The cumulative total over the 30 days would be over $10,000,000!)

Tip

Using pennies as manipulatives can help students visualize a pattern, as can coloring in boxes on graph paper.

Try This Too! Plus Two Pyramid

Help students understand the difference between doubling (multiplying by two) and just adding on two with this activity. Have students again track the earnings of a dishwasher over 30 days, this time adding two cents on each day rather than doubling the amount each day (as before). Students can use graph paper to work out their earnings, starting in the middle of the paper and then working out from there in a pyramid fashion. If students create the entire Plus Two Pyramid, they will have 900 squares. (They can add graph paper to accommodate the entire procedure.) Pretty impressive, but at a penny a square, not real valuable compared to the doubling effect.

Six-Dinner Sid

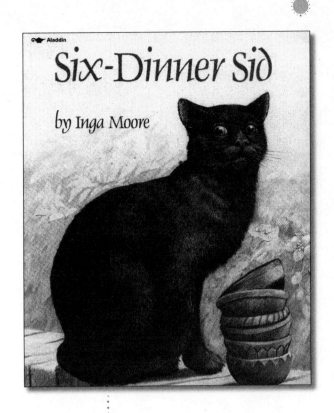

by Inga Moore (Simon & Schuster, 1991)

Sid is a cat that lives on Aristotle Street. He lives at #1 Aristotle Street, also at numbers 2, 3, 4, 5, and 6. Since nobody on the street talks to one another, Sid enjoys six dinners each night. This works well enough for Sid till he catches a cold and has to go to the vet—six times! The neighbors discover his clever plan and say that he will have only one dinner each night, whereupon Sid moves to Pythagoras Street and resumes his old pattern. However, on this street the neighbors talk to each other and know about Sid living with all six, and getting six dinners. But since they know, they don't mind, and everyone is happy.

Math Vocabulary

extend: to continue, stretch, or prolong

Sharing the Story

After reading the story, focus a discussion on the pattern of Sid's meals. He ate six dinners, one at each of the six houses where he lived. An easy way to represent patterns physically is with shapes. To have students practice pattern creation and extension, provide everyone with a copy of page 35. Have students cut out the shapes and use them to create three different patterns. Partner students and ask them to share and compare patterns. Partners should try to describe the patterns they see and extend the pattern, explaining what would come next.

NCTM STANDARDS

Algebra

Understand patterns, relations, and functions.

☼ Analyze how repeating and growing patterns are generated.

☼ Describe, extend, and make generalizations about geometric and numeric patterns.

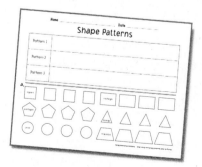

Six Dinner Sid's Weekly Chart

Students chart Sid's meals and discover how recognizing patterns can help them to arrive at answers quickly and easily.

Materials

☼ weekly chart (page 36)

☼ pencils

Tip

For everything your class might want to know about cats, check out *The Ultimate Cat Book* by David Taylor (Simon & Schuster, 1989), and the unusual *Purr...Children's Book Illustrators Brag About Their Cats*, edited by Michael Rosen (Harcourt Brace, 1996).

1. Invite students to pretend that they are a cat like Sid and move from house to house—living and eating in six different homes. Have students describe the pattern they see in the book: Sid gets one dinner at each of six houses each night. He repeated the pattern even when he moved. Give each child a copy of page 36. Review the pattern for one dinner a day at each of six houses.

2. Pose the question, "What if Sid were to get two meals a day?" Have students record this pattern on the chart. Discuss the result.

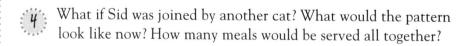

3. Ask students to think about what the patterns and totals would look like for three meals a day. Have them record this on the chart.

4. What if Sid was joined by another cat? What would the pattern look like now? How many meals would be served all together?

Try This Too! Valuable Bracelets

Both boys and girls at this level enjoy bracelets. Making them provides a good patterning activity that integrates other math concepts. Give students three colors of beads and a length of yarn. Assign a value to each color of bead—for example, white = 1 cent, red = 2 cents, blue = 10 cents. Give students a set amount of money. Ask them to design a bracelet with a color pattern they can describe, and a total cost. For a more complete version of this project, see *Special Delivery: Putting Math to Work* by Bob Krech (ETA/Cuisenaire, 1998).

Spaghetti and Meatballs for All!

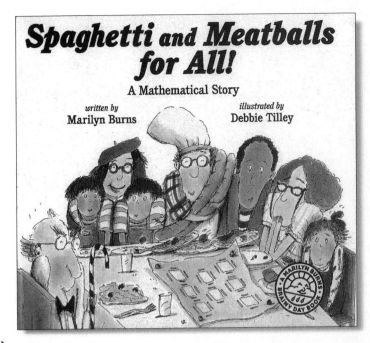

by Marilyn Burns (Scholastic Press, 1994)

Mr. and Mrs. Comfort are planning a family reunion. Mr. Comfort prepares plenty of food, and Mrs. Comfort has a plan for arranging all the tables and chairs. But as guests arrive, they rearrange the tables and chairs to accommodate newcomers and those they want to sit with. Mrs. Comfort begins to panic. There will not be enough seats for everyone!

Math Vocabulary

area: the number of square units needed to cover a figure

perimeter: the distance around a figure

trapezoid: a quadrilateral with one pair of parallel sides and one pair of sides that are not parallel

Sharing the Story

After reading the story, give students copies of the table and chair patterns on page 37. Have students cut them out, and arrange them in the original formation. Now re-read the story, pausing at each arrangement to let students re-create it with their manipulatives and record how many people could be seated. Discuss why the number of possible seats changes and why spaces are gained and lost.

Algebra

Understand patterns, relations, and functions.

* Sort, classify, and order objects by size, number, and other properties.

* Analyze, describe, and extend repeating and growing patterns.

Use mathematical models to represent and understand quantitative relationships.

* Model situations that involve addition and subtraction of whole numbers, using objects, pictures, and symbols.

Materials

- drawing paper
- construction paper
- scissors
- rulers
- glue

The Design Your New Classroom Contest

Mrs. Comfort designed a furniture arrangement to best accommodate all her guests for the big dinner. Your students can participate in a similar activity: designing a new classroom arrangement to try out.

1. Discuss Mrs. Comfort's plan for arranging the tables and chairs for the family reunion. Explain that in real life, interior designers do this with paper or computer manipulatives.

2. Have students work with partners to create a set of construction paper desk and chair manipulatives that reflect those in the classroom. Invite students to use their manipulatives to create a new design for the classroom. Encourage them to consider movement around the class, convenience, small and large meeting areas, and so on.

3. Let each team present their designs to the class, explaining the thinking behind the arrangements. You may want to conclude by having the class vote for a favorite design (or combine favorite elements from each for a new design), then try it out!

Try This Too!   Connecting Shapes

Provide students with a variety of attribute blocks, pattern blocks, or geoblocks. Ask students to measure the pieces in centimeters and record the perimeter and area of each. Now have them combine four shapes to create a new shape or design. All shapes must connect on at least one side. When the design is complete, have students measure the perimeter and area. How do their new measurements compare with the measurements of the individual pieces? What relationships do students see? Challenge children to create another design and predict the new perimeter and area. Experiment with writing equations that might help describe the patterns students see.

Shape Patterns

Pattern 1	Pattern 2	Pattern 3

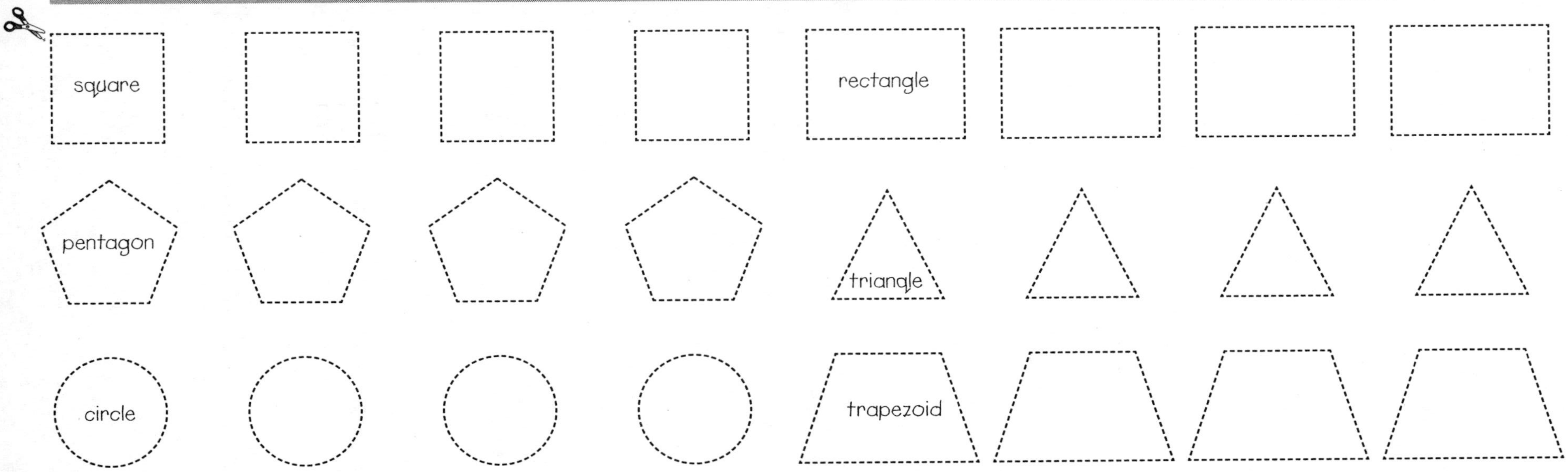

square

pentagon

circle

rectangle

triangle

trapezoid

Meeting the Math Standards With Favorite Picture Books   Scholastic Professional Books

Name _____

Date _____

Six-Dinner Sid's Weekly Chart

	Number of Dinners at Each House	Sunday	Monday	Tuesday	Wednesday	Thursday	Friday	Saturday	Weekly Total
Number of Houses									
6	1	6	6	6	6	6	6	6	42

Meeting the Math Standards With Favorite Picture Books   Scholastic Professional Books

Name _____ Date _____

Mrs. Comfort's
Tables and Chairs

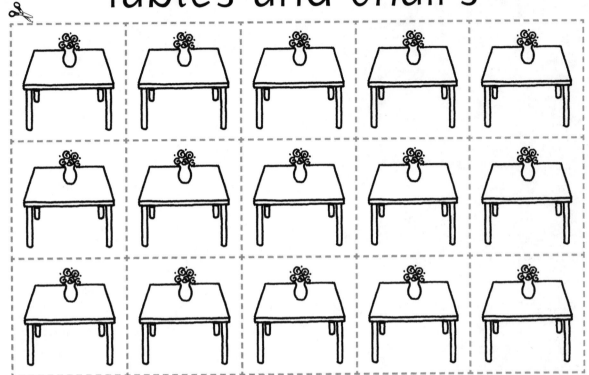

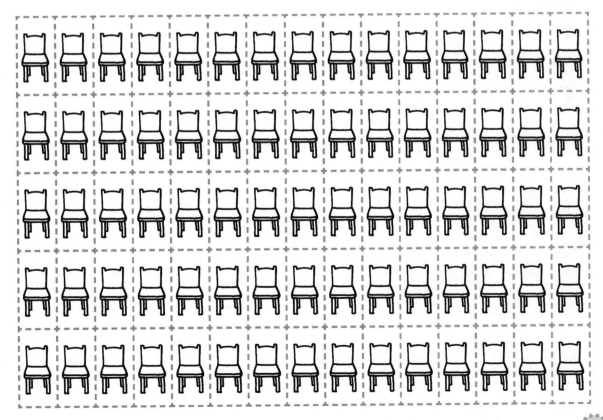

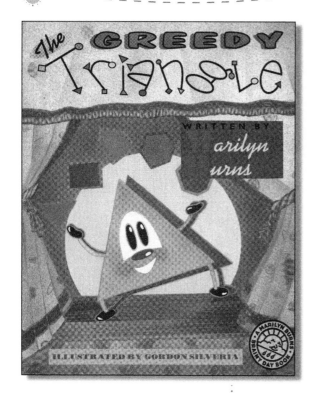

The Greedy Triangle

by Marilyn Burns (Scholastic, 1994)

The triangle in this story is very busy. He does lots of things, like perform in an orchestra, hold up bridges, and catch the wind for sailboats, but he is dissatisfied and wants to try new things. The triangle pays a visit to the local shape-shifter, who grants him his request of adding one more side and one more angle, which makes him a quadrilateral. But he's still not satisfied and continues adding sides and angles until finally, he is almost round and rolls out of control. Being a triangle seems like a good idea after all.

Math Vocabulary

attribute: an inherent property such as color, shape, size
polygon: a closed plane figure made up of line segments
quadrilateral: a polygon with four sides
triangle: a polygon with three sides

Sharing the Story

One of the most important things we can allow children to do as they begin exploring shapes is to let them create their own definitions for the shapes they learn about. After reading the story, say, "We heard about a lot of different shapes in that book. For example, the main character is a triangle. I'm sure most of you have heard of a triangle, but exactly what is a triangle? Let's see if we can write a definition for it." Work with students to write several statements that describe a triangle. Use this as a model for defining a variety of shapes for a class reference chart.

NCTM STANDARDS

Geometry

Analyze characteristics and properties of two- and three-dimensional shapes.

- ☼ Recognize, name, build, draw, compare, and sort two- and three-dimensional shapes.

- ☼ Describe attributes and parts of two- and three-dimensional shapes.

Use visualization, spatial reasoning, and geometric modeling to solve problems.

- ☼ Build and draw geometric shapes.

- ☼ Recognize geometric shapes in the environment.

Shape Family Portrait

Students explore geometry by creating single-shape portraits.

1. Give each student a sheet of drawing paper. Make plenty of crayons, markers, pencils, and rulers available.

2. Review the many different shapes introduced in the book. List these on the chalkboard along with a rendering of each.

3. Explain that students will be creating an unusual "family portrait." This portrait will include many members of the Shape Family.

4. Provide the materials and assign a shape to each student (or pair). Ask students to create a portrait of their Shape Family member using only that shape—for example, the square member of the family can be made of only squares (square nose, square eyes, square feet, and so on).

5. Encourage students to name their family member according to the shape—for example, Timmy Triangle and Helen Hexagon. Arrange the portraits on a bulletin board to create a Shape Family display.

Materials

- drawing paper (at least 11 by 17 inches)
- pencils, crayons, markers
- rulers
- construction paper
- scissors
- glue

Try This Too! Possible Polygons

When children start learning about polygons, they begin to ask questions, such as "What do you call a 16-sided polygon?" Use their curiosity as the basis of a daily or weekly challenge. First, go to **www.mathforum.com/dr.math/** for a list of all the possible polygons your students will ever entertain. Write the name of one on the chalkboard, and challenge students to find out what it is and create it on a geoboard or geodot paper.

Sir Cumference and the First Round Table

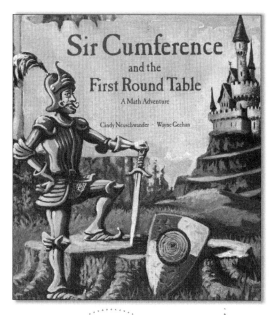

by Cindy Neuschwander (Charlesbridge, 1997)

King Arthur calls his knights together as it appears an attack is imminent. They meet at the long rectangular table as usual. Sir Cumference, one of the knights, complains to his wife, Lady Di of Ameter, that his throat is sore from yelling to be heard at the other end of the table. She suggests cutting the table in two and arranging the pieces to form a square. Problems result and the table is redesigned again and again, resulting in a parallelogram, triangle, oval, and so on, each of which has its own problems. Finally a circle shape is decided upon and The Knights of the Round Table are born.

Math Vocabulary

circle: a plane figure in which all points are equidistant from the center

circumference: the distance around a circle

diameter: a line segment that goes from a point on a circle through the center to another point on the circle

radius: a line from the center of a circle to any point on the circle

Sharing the Story

After reading the story, review the definitions of circumference, radius, and diameter. Invite students to brainstorm everyday objects that might need to be measured in this way—for example, pipes, plates, and wheels. Bring in some of the objects you discuss for students to measure.

Geometry

Analyze characteristics and properties of two- and three-dimensional shapes.

☼ Recognize, name, build, draw, compare, and sort 2-D and 3-D shapes.

☼ Describe attributes of 2-D and 3-D shapes.

Use visualization, spatial reasoning, and geometric modeling to solve problems.

☼ Recognize geometric shapes in the environment.

Table Designs

Diameter, radius, and circumference are discussed in the story, and are, of course, named after the heroic trio who helped create the new table. Let students experiment with their own table designs. They'll have fun naming their new shapes, too.

Materials

❋ one-centimeter graph paper

❋ pencils

1 Look back at the book together and list on the chalkboard the various shapes the knights tried for their table.

2 Give each child a sheet of centimeter graph paper. Ask students to draw on their paper and label the shapes from the story.

3 Now give each student another sheet of graph paper. Have students create a new table shape for the knights. It could be a combination of the shapes discussed or a shape not yet considered.

4 After drawing their table shape, ask students to write a few sentences explaining the benefits of the shape. Let students give their new table shape a name, incorporating the geometry of their design in the name.

It's the rectangle H table.

A lot of people can sit at my table.

JASON

Learn More! Good Knight!

Take a look at *Eyewitness Books: Knight* by Christopher Gravett (Knopf, 1993), chock full of illustrations and photos for everything you ever wanted to know about knights. As students look over the book, suggest that they watch for decorative designs that use geometric shapes on armor, shields, banners, and castles. Then invite students to use what they know about geometry to create their own shield or banner designs based on these shapes.

The Village of Round and Square Houses

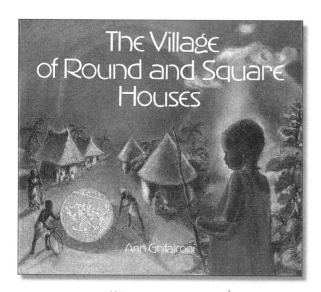

by Ann Grifalconi (Little, Brown, 1986)

A young girl recounts her grandmother's tale of how it came to be that in a village in Africa, the men live in square houses and the women live in round ones.

Math Vocabulary

cone: a 3-D figure with one curved surface, one flat surface (usually circular), one curved edge, and one vertex

cube: a regular solid having six congruent square faces

face: a flat surface on a solid figure

rectangular prism: a solid figure whose six faces are all rectangles

round: every part of the surface is equidistant from the center

square: a quadrilateral that has four equal sides and four right angles

three-dimensional: having length, width, and height

triangular prism: a prism with triangular bases

two-dimensional: having length and width

Sharing the Story

Either before or after reading the story, give each student a sheet of drawing paper to take home. Ask students to draw the shapes that make up the structure of their home and record the names of the shapes. As a followup, ask students why they think those shapes were selected to create the structures. For example, what is the advantage of a triangular roof or square wall? This is a good step toward encouraging students to think about the purposeful use of geometry in their environment.

NCTM STANDARDS

Geometry

Analyze characteristics and properties of two- and three-dimensional shapes.

☼ Recognize, name, build, draw, compare, and sort 2-D and 3-D shapes.

Use visualization, spatial reasoning, and geometric modeling to solve problems.

☼ Build and draw geometric shapes, and recognize them in the environment.

☼ Identify and build a 3-D object from 2-D representations.

The Village the Class Built

Students may notice that the houses in *The Village of Round and Square Houses* are not actually circles or squares. The structures are supposed to be three-dimensional, so are in fact made with cubes, cylinders, cones, and pyramids. Students will have fun creating these shapes to explore the relationship between 2-D and 3-D objects.

Materials

☼ cardboard

☼ clay

☼ craft sticks

1. The relationship between two-dimensional shapes and three-dimensional shapes is an interesting one. An example is the cube, which has six square sides or faces that together make a three-dimensional shape. Invite students to list 2-D shapes they know—for example, square, triangle, and rectangle. Now ask students to think about related 3-D shapes—for example, square/cube, triangle/pyramid, and rectangle/rectangular prism. Record these on a class chart.

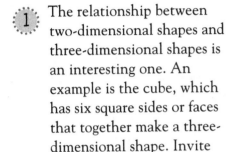

2. Have students explore these relationships on their own with clay. Give each student a small cardboard base, clay, and a craft stick. Ask students to use the materials to create 3-D clay structures that incorporate all of the shapes on the chart and any others they might know of or learn about.

3. Let students work together to create a village with their structures. Have them take turns identifying the two- and three-dimensional shapes they used.

Try This Too! 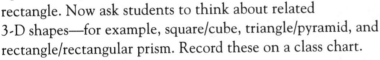 ## Straw Sculptures

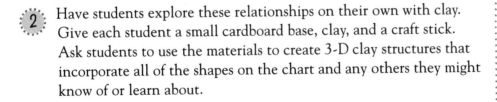

Share *The History of Western Sculpture: A Young Person's Guide* (Steck-Vaughn, 1996). This book provides clear text and photo illustrations to help students learn about sculpture. Focus particularly on the section on twentieth-century sculpture, where students can find numerous examples of pieces based entirely on geometric shapes. Provide students with clay, straws, and scissors. Invite students to cut the straws to suitable lengths and join them with clay to create 3-D sculptures.

Grandfather Tang's Story

by Ann Tompert (Crown, 1990)

Grandfather Tang and Little Soo amuse themselves by making different shapes with their tangram puzzles. They use their shapes to tell a story about two foxes, Chou and Wu Ling, who use their magic powers to change into various animals. Grandpa and Soo portray the animals and their adventures with their tangram pieces.

Math Vocabulary

tangram: an ancient seven-piece Chinese puzzle

Sharing the Story

Obtain multiple copies of the book or take turns passing the book around to groups of four or five students. Assign one part of the story and one tangram animal to each group. Have students copy the words from their part of the story on the back of a large sheet of paper. On the front of the paper, have them make a large tangram of their animal character. (They can use the tangram shapes on page 46 or create their own larger ones.) After groups have practiced individually, have all groups read their sections and show their tangrams in order to perform the entire story.

Tangram Stories

Materials

* tangram patterns (page 46)
* colored paper
* scissors
* pencils
* glue

Like Grandfather and Soo, children use tangrams to create characters and tell their own stories.

1. In "Sharing the Story" students followed along with illustrations from *Grandfather Tang's Story* and used their tangrams to re-create the book's pictures.

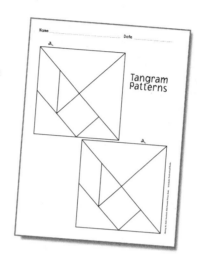

2. Have students go further by using tangram pieces to make their own character—an animal, person, or object. Encourage creativity! The only rule is that they can only use the seven standard pieces.

3. To get started, give each child a copy of the tangram shapes on page 46. Have children cut out the pieces and then experiment with an arrangement. When they are satisfied with their figure, have them glue the pieces in place on a sheet of colored paper.

4. Ask students to write a short story that goes with their tangram. Or, have children work in groups and combine their characters into one collaborative story. Provide time for students to share and display their stories.

Try This Too! Tangram Challenge

Have students cut out the tangram shapes on page 46 and trace them on oaktag. Let students use the shapes to make various tangram designs (again using the seven pieces). Have them outline their design (then remove the actual shape cutouts) to make puzzles for classmates to solve (by trying to fit their tangram pieces in the shape to replicate the design).

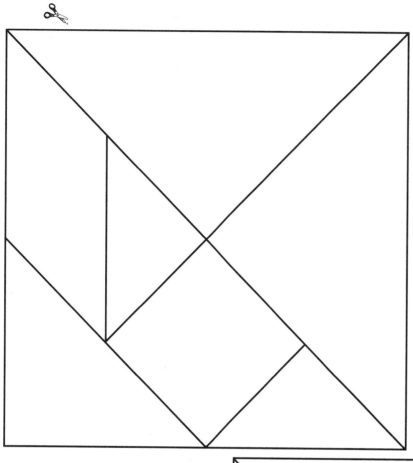

Tangram
Patterns

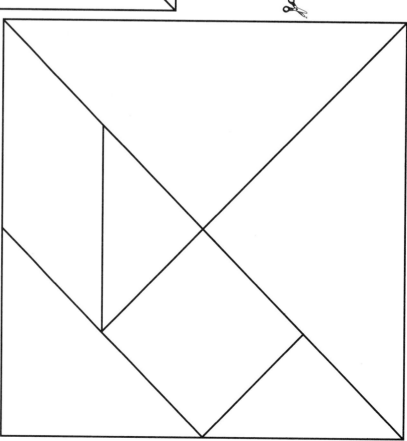

Meeting the Math Standards With Favorite Picture Books   Scholastic Professional Books

Measuring Penny

by Loreen Leedy (Holiday House, 1997)

Lisa's teacher gives the class an interesting homework assignment. He asks his students to go home and measure something: a sofa, a television set, a doll—anything. They are to measure it in as many ways as they can (height, width, length, weight, volume, temperature, time), record the results, and do at least one comparison. When Lisa gets home she is greeted by her dog, Penny. She immediately decides that Penny will be the "something" she measures for homework.

Math Vocabulary

estimate: to find a number close to an exact amount

height: the perpendicular distance from the base to the top

length: the distance along a line or figure from one point to another

volume: the number of cubic units of space a solid figure takes up

weight: a measure of how heavy an object is

Sharing the Story

Mr. Jayson created a great homework assignment. Why not use it with your class as well? Read aloud Mr. Jayson's assignment asking students to measure something in as many ways as they can. When students return their papers, have them share their measurements with the class, without revealing what they measured. See if the rest of the students can guess what the item is based on the measurements given. This activity helps expand students' understanding of measurement and builds real-life connections.

NCTM STANDARDS

Measurement

Understand measurable attributes of objects and the units, systems, and processes of measurement.

- Recognize attributes of length, volume, weight, area, and time.

- Measure using nonstandard and standard units.

Apply appropriate techniques, tools, and formulas to determine measurements.

- Use tools and common referents to estimate, measure, and compare.

Estimation Stations

Discuss the idea that one of the most important aspects of working with measurement is to build estimation skills. Let students suggest real-life situations in which they might not have measuring tools handy and would need to estimate. Set up these estimation stations to learn more.

Materials

- ☼ index cards
- ☼ record sheet (page 55)
- ☼ bathroom scales
- ☼ postal scales
- ☼ rulers
- ☼ measuring tapes
- ☼ yardsticks
- ☼ thermometers
- ☼ timers

1. Divide the class into groups of three or four. Let each group choose an object to measure. (If it's an object from home, students will need to be able to bring it in.)

2. Have students in each group measure their item as many ways as they can—for example, height, weight, length, volume, temperature, and time—and record the data on an index card.

3. When all groups have completed their data cards, set up an estimation station for each item. Give each student a copy of page 55. Have students rotate in their groups to each station to make and record estimates for each item. Encourage students to discuss differences in their estimates. Note that they do not have to agree.

4. Add measurement tools to each station. Let students revisit the stations to make and record actual measurements for each item.

5. Have students compare their measurements to those recorded on the data cards and calculate the differences between their estimates and the actual measurements. As practice with measurements continues, try this activity again with a new set of items and focus on how students' estimates become more accurate with practice.

Try This Too!   Big Dogs, Small Dogs

Read *Dogs* by Gail Gibbons (Holiday House, 1996). In a simple, colorful style, Gibbons provides good basic information about dogs, including facts about anatomy, breeds, and communication as well as the basics about care and feeding. Ask students to see if they can find any measurement information about dogs in Gibbons's book or other sources. Which dogs grow to be the largest? How large? Which are the smallest? How small? Brainstorm questions like these and assign them to small research groups that will report back to the class with their measurement findings.

How Big Is a Foot?

by Rolf Myller (Dell, 1962)

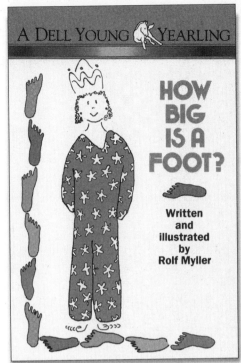

I t's the Queen's birthday. But what can the King give someone who has everything? A bed! (They hadn't been invented yet.) The King uses his feet to measure how big the bed should be. Unfortunately the carpenter making the bed has feet that are much smaller, and a very small bed results. The apprentice eventually figures out that he needs to use the King's foot for the measurement. The King helps out by having a sculptor carve a foot that is the same size, which of course becomes the standard measure throughout the kingdom.

Math Vocabulary

nonstandard measurement: measuring with units other than customary or metric units

standard measurement: measurement using customary or metric units

Sharing the Story

Let students experience the idea of standard measurement for themselves by inviting them to measure the room (from one end to the other) in their feet. They can count off the feet as they walk heel to toe from one end to the other or trace their feet and use the cutouts as a measurement. Have students compare their measurements. Why are there differences? What's the range? Let them estimate the same distance if they used a ruler, then try it out.

NCTM STANDARDS

Measurement

Understand measurable attributes of objects and the units, systems, and processes of measurement.

- Recognize attributes of length, volume, weight, area, and time.

- Measure using nonstandard and standard units.

- Understand the need for standard units.

Apply appropriate techniques, tools, and formulas to determine measurements.

- Use tools and common referents to estimate, measure, and compare.

- rulers
- yardsticks
- measuring tapes
- pencils
- paper
- chart paper

Biggest Thing in the School!

Here's a measurement investigation that piques students' curiosity and gives them an opportunity for some big-time hands-on measurement.

1. Ask students, "What do you think the biggest thing in the school is?" Common responses include a teacher's desk, the boiler, a cafeteria table, and the principal! Record ideas on the chalkboard and then ask, "How big do you think each is?" Record estimates.

2. From the ideas listed on the chalkboard, select five for investigation. Organize students into five groups and supply each group with a ruler, yardstick, measuring tape, pencil, and sheet of paper.

3. Take students on mini–field trips to measure each item. You may want to measure one a day for five days. Have each group make and record measurements for their assigned item.

4. Compile students' data on chart paper. Encourage students to make comparisons, then answer the question: "What is the biggest thing in the school?"

Try This Too! A Small Measure

Bring in a collection of small items from home or ask students to do so. As students look over these items, ask them to try to find things that are smaller in length than an inch. Have them use a ruler to measure the lengths of these items, then order them from shortest to longest. Discuss the fractional segments of an inch on the ruler and work together to identify these marks. Repeat the activity using the centimeter side of the ruler. Compare both sets of measurements and ask, "Are there times when it is better to use centimeters? Are there times when it is better to use inches?"

America's Champion Swimmer: Gertrude Ederle

by David Adler (Harcourt, 2000)

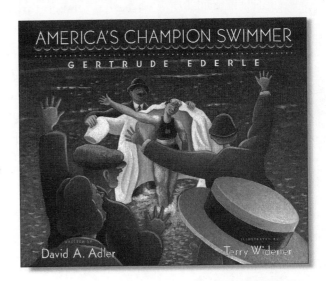

This true story follows the life of Gertrude Ederle from her birth in 1906. We hear how her father taught her to swim after he found out that she nearly drowned in a pond. After she learned to swim, it was hard to keep Gertrude out of the water. She became a champion swimmer, participating in the Olympics and becoming the first woman to swim the English Channel. (In fact, she beat the men's record by almost two hours!) She was an inspiration then, and continues to be so today.

Math Vocabulary

temperature: a measure of hotness or coldness

thermometer: an instrument used for measuring temperature

Sharing the Story

When reading the story, remind students that Gertrude Ederle often swam against the clock. Timing of swimming events lets us know who the winner is. To reinforce this idea, help students create their own personal Olympics. Give each student a copy of page 56. Have students choose and record events they would like to try— for example, running 50 yards, hopping 20 yards on one foot, and walking backward 10 yards. Have students time each other as they try to break their personal records over a period of four weeks. Make sure to allow some practice and training time in between attempts. Work with students to read stopwatches, wristwatches, and clocks with accuracy, and discuss how to record times.

Measurement

Understand measurable attributes of objects and the units, systems, and processes of measurement.

- Recognize attributes of length, volume, weight, area, and time.

- Measure using nonstandard and standard units.

- Understand the need for standard units.

Apply appropriate techniques, tools, and formulas to determine measurements.

Taking the School's Temperature

One of the difficult things Gertrude Ederle had to overcome was the freezing temperatures of the water in the English Channel. With this activity, children explore temperature—an attribute they can measure.

Materials

- record sheet (page 57)
- small thermometers
- tape
- markers
- chart paper

1. The unmarked lines on a thermometer can be confusing. Comparing the thermometer to a vertical number line can help. Make this connection for students, then brainstorm with students why these lines are not numbered. (All the numbers don't fit on a small instrument.)

2. Give students some practice reading a thermometer. Once they are comfortable reading thermometers, try this experiment. Assign pairs of students various rooms throughout the school. Tape a small thermometer in each of these rooms by the door. Send students in pairs each day at the same time to record the temperature of the rooms. Give them a copy of page 57 to record results.

3. Chart and compare the results for each room. Ask, "Which room is coldest? Which is hottest? Why do you think this is so?" Encourage students to think about real-life connections that affect temperature in a building, such as windows, high ceilings, location, and direction of sun.

Try This Too! How Fast? How Far? How High?

Ask students to choose a sport to investigate with an emphasis on measurement. Using newspapers, reference books, the Internet, magazines, and other available sources, have students find out what aspects of measurement are used in that sport. For example, in football both time and length are important. The game is timed in minutes and seconds. The field is marked off in yards. Give students a copy of page 58 and have them record their information.

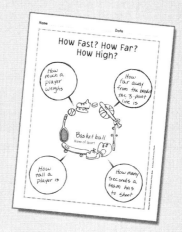

Arthur's Pet Business

by Marc Brown (Little, Brown, 1990)

Arthur wants a pet and asks his parents if he can get one, but like most parents they want some proof that Arthur is ready and responsible enough to have a pet. To prove that he is responsible, Arthur starts his own pet business; he takes care of other people's pets for a fee. He learns to take care of pets, earns some money, and proves himself to his parents. In the end one of his clients has a litter of puppies and Arthur is awarded one by the owner. His parents agree that he may keep the puppy. He has proven that he is ready to have his own pet.

Math Vocabulary

skip-counting: counting by multiples of a number (for example, 2, 4, 6, 8...)

Sharing the Story

In Arthur's story, just as in real life, time and money are closely related. Ask the class to think about Arthur's business. He took care of quite a few pets. Have small groups discuss what a reasonable price for an hour of pet care would be. Now estimate together how many hours Arthur cared for the various pets in the book. List all the pets and the estimated hours. Calculate how much money Arthur would have earned with these figures.

Measurement

Understand measurable attributes of objects and the units, systems, and processes of measurement.

* Recognize the attributes of time.

* Understand the need for measuring with standard units.

Apply appropriate techniques, tools, and formulas to determine measurements.

* Use tools and common referents to estimate, measure, and compare.

Schedule It! Live It!

Materials

☀ lined paper

☀ pencils

☀ play clocks (optional)

Arthur had to set up a schedule to take care of all the various pets he worked with. This activity gives students some practice scheduling classroom time and then applying the schedule with very exciting results.

1. At the beginning of the day, list the schedule for the class day ahead. For each activity, note the anticipated beginning time, ending time, and elapsed time. Ask students how this schedule might help you. (It helps you plan the day, organize time, accomplish goals, make sure students get to their specials, and so on.) Repeat this procedure for a few days.

2. Choose an upcoming day when you have some flexibility. Write the date on the board. Tell students that this date will be special. It will be a day that students will determine the schedule and "live it!"

3. On the chalkboard, write activities with times that can't change for the day—for example, lunch time, specials, and arrival and dismissal. Divide the class into groups of four or five and provide each with lined paper, pencils, and manipulative clocks if needed. Ask each group to develop a schedule of activities for the class on the chosen day, including the required activities and adding their own to fill out the day. Remind students that choices must be reasonable and do-able, and that for each they must include the beginning, ending, and elapsed time.

4. Invite groups to write their schedule on the chalkboard and present them to the class. Vote on a favorite or negotiate a schedule that combines favorite elements of each. Have children copy the schedule on paper, then when the day comes, live it! Students will be so excited to have applied their knowledge of time in a real way.

Try This Too! On Schedule

In *Bats Around the Clock* by Kathi Appelt (HarperCollins, 2000), Click Dark is the batty host of American Batstand, a 12-hour rock-and-roll television extravaganza. Every hour of Click's show the bats do a new dance or hear a new performer. As a followup, ask students to bring in printed material that includes a scheduled time—for example, TV schedules, sports schedules, train schedules, and party invitations. Ask each student to share an example with the class and explain why time is an important consideration.

Name ———————————— Date ————————————

Estimation Stations

Estimation = E
Measurement = M

Object	Height	Weight	Length	Volume	Temperature
1	E ——— M ———	E ——— M ———	E ——— M ———	E ——— M ———	E ——— M ———
2	E ——— M ———	E ——— M ———	E ——— M ———	E ——— M ———	E ——— M ———
3	E ——— M ———	E ——— M ———	E ——— M ———	E ——— M ———	E ——— M ———

Name _____

Date _____

Personal Olympics

Event	Week 1	Week 2	Week 3	Week 4

Meeting the Math Standards With Favorite Picture Books · Scholastic Professional Books

Taking the School's Temperature

Date	Time	Temp.	Date	Time	Temp.

How Fast? How Far? How High?

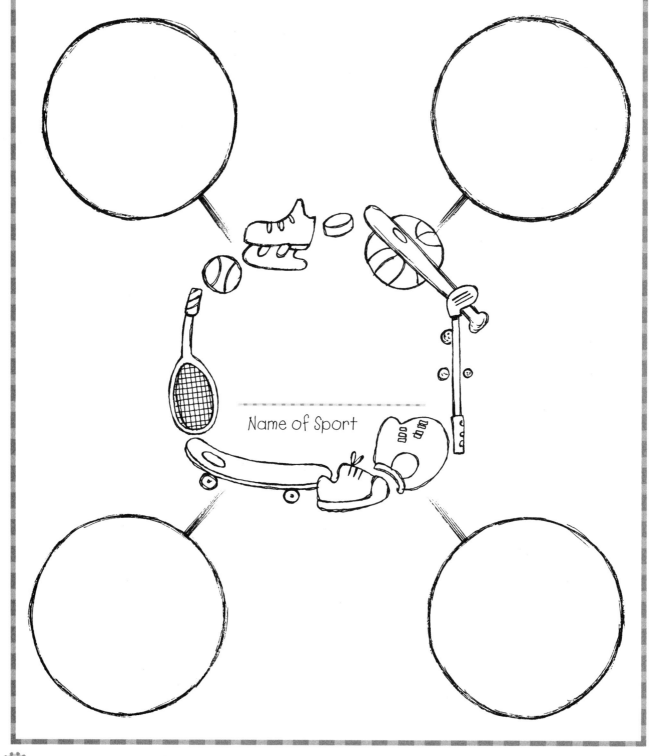

Name of Sport

A Three Hat Day

by Laura Geringer (Harper and Row, 1985)

RR Pottle III's father collected canes, and his mother collected umbrellas. He collects hats and selects his hat (or hats) each day before he even yawns. He feels depressed though, because he has not yet found his true love. But as he sets off on a dreary day with three hats on (to cheer himself up) he finds his true love, where else? In a hat store. Their daughter, RR Pottle IV, becomes, what else? A collector of shoes.

Math Vocabulary

combination: a group of items or events; changing the order does not create a new combination

probability: the chance of an event happening

Sharing the Story

After reading the story, remind the class that Mr. Pottle had a lot of hats to choose from. He sometimes wore them in combinations, two or three at a time. Of course, he also wore other items of clothing as well. Give each student a copy of page 65, which includes a variety of hats and ties Mr. Pottle might wear. Have students use the hat and tie patterns as manipulatives to figure out the possible combinations that exist. For example, if he has on three of the hats and two ties, how many possible combinations are there? As students work they may discover that by multiplying the number of hats used by the number of ties, they can figure out the total number of possible combinations without even using the manipulatives.

NCTM STANDARDS

Data Analysis and Probability

Formulate questions and collect, organize, and display relevant data to answer them.

※ Sort and classify objects.

※ Represent data using concrete objects, pictures, and graphs.

Understand and apply basic concepts of probability.

※ Discuss the degree of likelihood of events using words such as *certain, equally likely,* and *impossible.*

※ Predict outcomes of simple experiments and test predictions.

Pottle's Probability

Pose this question to students: Mr. Pottle chose to wear certain hats on certain days, but what if he wanted to use the element of chance in his hat-wearing decisions? Try this activity to find out!

1. Give each student a copy of page 66. There are 30 hats on the page. Have everyone color five hats blue and the rest red and then cut them out. Place the hat patterns in a real hat.

2. Ask students to predict what color hat you will pull out in this little experiment. Have them explain their reasoning. The likelihood is that the hat will be red. There is a greater probability, because there is a greater number of red hats. Encourage the use of probability terms, such as *certain*, *impossible*, and *likely*. Describe possibilities with expressions, such as "There's a one in five chance when there is one red hat in a set of five."

3. Divide the class into groups of three or four students. Distribute a mixed set of precut red and blue hats to each group as well as a real hat to hold the paper ones. Give some groups a greater number of red hats, some a greater number of blue, and some an even number of blue and red.

4. Have students count and record the number of red and blue hats they have, then place them in the hat and mix them up. Ask them to predict what color hat they will pull out first, then record their results. Have students repeat this for a given number of trials.

5. Invite students in each group to share their results, with a focus on probability.

Try This Too!

My Many Outfits

Provide students with copies of clothing catalogs from the mail or stores. Tell students to imagine they each have $100 to spend. You want them to create a collection of pants and shirts that will provide the greatest number of possible combinations of outfits to wear. Using the catalogs and working in small groups, have students create a list of the items they would buy, the individual prices, colors, and total cost. Then have them find all the possible combinations using the clothes they chose to purchase.

The Best Vacation Ever

by Stuart J. Murphy (HarperCollins, 1997)

In rhyming prose we learn about a young girl's busy family. They all need a vacation but can't decide where to go. To help with this dilemma the girl takes a survey and charts the results of the family preferences. She draws up various charts to find out if people want to be somewhere warm or cool, far or near, fun or quiet, and so on. She tallies up her results and finds that the best possible vacation spot is camping in their own backyard.

Math Vocabulary

data: information, especially numerical information; usually organized for analysis

survey: the process of asking a group of people the same question

Sharing the Story

Before reading the story, have students bring in newspapers and look for displays of data—for example, in the sports pages and weather reports. *USA Today* makes particular use of graphs on their front page to convey information, often the results of opinion polls. Have each student cut out a data display from a newspaper and paste it on a sheet of lined paper. Ask students to make at least two statements about the data and explain how they believe the data display supports these statements. After reading the story, ask the class how many of the data displays they found were based on a survey like the one in the story.

Data Analysis and Probability

Formulate questions and collect, organize, and display relevant data to answer them.

- ☼ Pose questions and collect data using observations, surveys, and experiments.

- ☼ Represent data using tables and graphs.

Use appropriate methods to analyze data.

Understand and apply basic concepts of probability.

- ☼ Describe the likelihood of events using words such as *certain, equally likely,* and *impossible.*

- ☼ Predict outcomes of simple experiments and test predictions.

Parking Lot Data

- ☼ paper
- ☼ pencils, crayons, markers
- ☼ drawing paper
- ☼ art supplies

Most schools have parking lots. Believe it or not, this can be a rich source of data.

1. Take a walk with your students to the parking lot. Have students work with a partner to write down attributes of cars in the lot—for example, types of license plates, color, two or four door, convertible or hardtop, and make.

2. Now have partners decide on an aspect of the parking lot they wish to collect and analyze data on. For example, some students might want to chart the number of cars in the lot over a one- or two-week period. Others might want to keep track of the car makes and see which make of car shows up the most.

3. Take a walk to the lot each day and let students collect data on their question. When all the results are in, have students graph or represent their data and post these displays on a bulletin board titled "Everything you always wanted to know about our parking lot, but were afraid to ask."

Try This Too!   ## Survey Says

Surveys are fun and interesting for students. Ask students to select a survey question and record it at the top of a sheet of paper. Have students decide whether the question will be multiple choice, yes or no, or open ended. Give everyone an opportunity to collect data by interviewing fellow students. Demonstrate how to use tally marks to record responses. As students complete their surveys, have them select a way to represent the data and share it with the class. Bar graphs, pictographs, and Venn diagrams are all possibilities.

If You Give a Mouse a Cookie

by Laura Joffe Numeroff (Harper and Row, 1985)

A young boy lures a mouse into his house with a cookie. Of course the mouse then wants some milk, and he'll probably ask for a straw, and then need a napkin . . . One thing leads to another until the boy's whole day is basically spent taking care of the mouse. At the end of the day the mouse is tired, thirsty, and hungry. So he'll probably want a glass of milk . . . and a cookie to go with it.

Math Vocabulary

chance: the likelihood that something will happen
likelihood: the chance of a certain thing happening
predict: to state or tell about what you believe will happen

Sharing the Story

Read the story and ask students to recall words that relate to probability, the study of chance, and the likelihood that things are going to happen—for example, *probably, if,* and *chances are.* Discuss how we know something will "probably" happen: We rely on previous knowledge and experience. That's why it's important to pay attention to the way things happen around you! It helps build knowledge that we can draw on to make predictions and decisions. Have students write three predictions using the word *probably,* including in each the reason they believe the prediction to be true—for example, "I think it will probably rain tonight because it has been cloudy all day."

NCTM STANDARDS

Data Analysis and Probability

Use appropriate methods to analyze data.

☼ Describe parts of the data and the set of data as a whole to determine what the data show.

Develop and evaluate inferences and predictions that are based on data.

☼ Discuss events related to students' experiences as likely or unlikely.

Understand and apply basic concepts of probability.

☼ Predict the probability of outcomes of simple experiments and test the predictions.

Cookie Spinners

Students make and test predictions with chocolate and vanilla cookie spinners.

Cookie Spinners

Materials

- cookie spinners (page 67)
- paper clips
- pencils

1. Make a copy of page 67 for each student. Show students how to use a paper clip and pencil to complete the spinner. (See illustration, right.)

2. Explain that the dark part of the cookie spinner is chocolate and the white part is vanilla. Have students predict the likelihood of which flavor will win in a spinning contest. Invite them to explain their reasoning.

3. Let students work with a partner to test their predictions. First, limit the experiment to two trials and have students record the results. Ask if that is a fair assessment.

4. It will be obvious to students that they need multiple trials in order to build up enough data to reasonably make predictions. Have students repeat the test with more trials this time, recording their results and comparing them to their predictions.

Tip

Let students create their own spinners, modeled after the cookie spinners. For example, they might make spinners with pizza toppings, ice cream flavors, or candy bars.

Try This Too! Games Show-and-Tell

Ask students to bring in a board game or card game from home. Tell them to be prepared to share briefly about their game: what the objective is, how it is played, and whether it involves probability and chance. Compare games. Ask: "Do some require more luck than others? Can we make predictions as we play based on what happens during the game?" After discussion, spend some time playing the games and then compare notes again.

Mr. Pottle's Hats and Ties

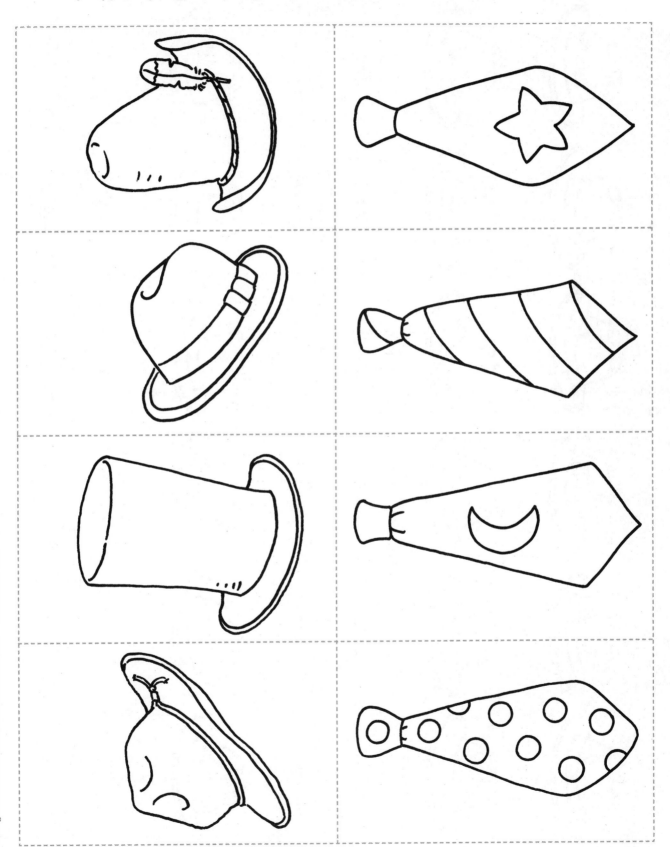

Pottle's Probability

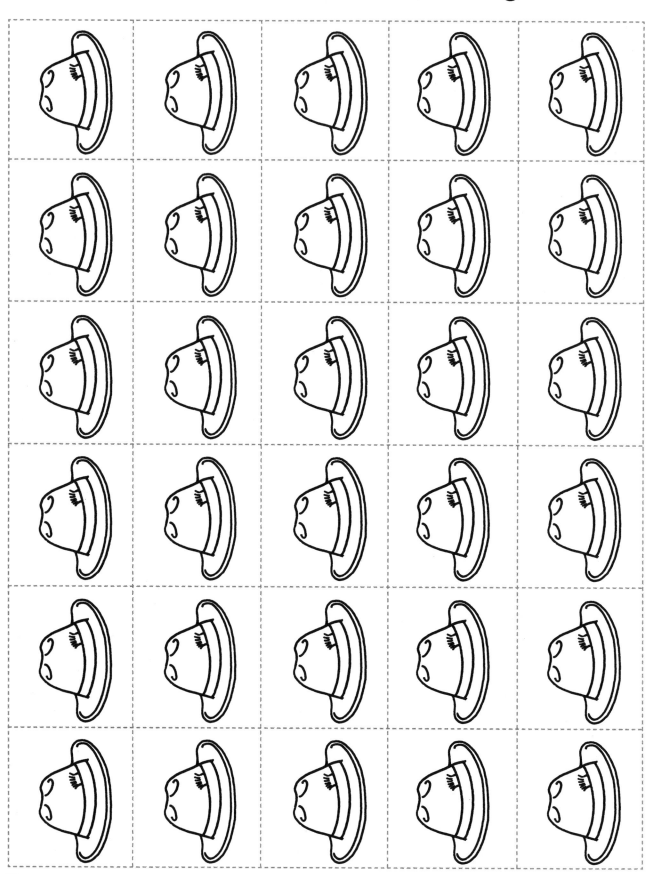

Cookie Spinners

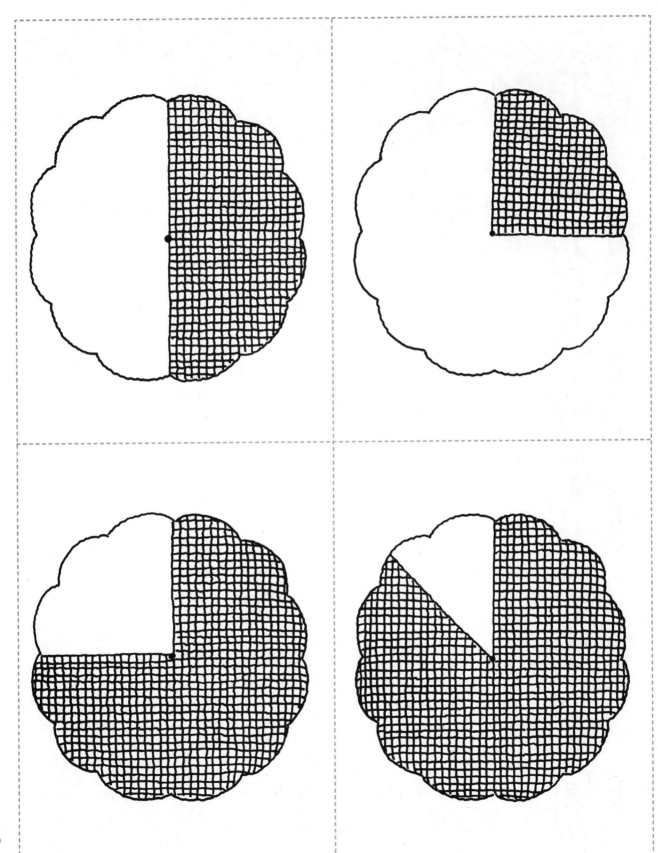

Math Curse

by Jon Scieszka and Lane Smith
(Viking, 1995)

On Monday in math class, Mrs. Fibonacci says, "You know, you can think of almost everything as a math problem." After that the young hero of the story begins to see math problems everywhere. Indeed, every aspect of his life becomes a math problem. This reaches frightening proportions until he dreams that he is trapped in a room with a lifetime of problems. Fortunately, he is clever enough to use his math knowledge and wit to escape and rid himself of the math curse. Unfortunately, in science the next day, Mrs. Newton suggest that almost everything can be thought of as a science experiment . . . .

Math Vocabulary

distracter: something that will sidetrack or distract attention
proof: evidence establishing the truth or validity of something
reasoning: coming to a conclusion based on logical thinking

Sharing the Story

Everywhere the boy in *Math Curse* turns there is another problem. Of course, he carried it to hilarious extremes. After reading the book, challenge students to identify math in their lives that they could write in problem format. Once each student writes a problem (and solves it), have students trade papers and try to work out each other's problems. You may want to theme these—for example, assigning topics such as math problems about school or a baseball team. Collect students' problems and put the pages together to make a book. Let children take it home to solve some of the problems with their families.

NCTM STANDARDS

Problem Solving

Use problem solving to build mathematical knowledge.

☀ Apply various strategies to solve problems that arise in mathematics and other contexts.

Reasoning and Proof

Recognize reasoning and proof as fundamental aspects of mathematics.

☀ Investigate mathematical conjectures.

☀ Select and use various types of reasoning and methods of proof.

Wacky Math Fill-Ins

Kids love playing Mad Libs. Here's a fun activity that combines a Mad Lib-like approach with math to create some very interesting (and sometimes hilarious) word problems.

Materials

* sample Mad Lib (optional)
* math fill-ins (page 74)
* pencils

1. If possible, try a Mad Lib with the class, letting students take turns supplying the missing parts of speech. Read the resulting story and let children have a good laugh. Then explain that they'll be doing the same sort of thing to make up math problems.

2. Before passing out copies of page 74, write the first problem on the chalkboard. Let students take turns supplying the parts of speech and missing numbers, then solve the problem together.

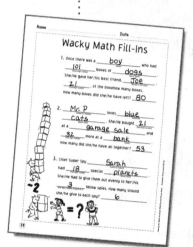

3. Assign each child a partner. Have partners sit facing each other. Give one student in each team a copy of page 74, with the paper folded so that only the first problem appears. Have students complete the problem like a Mad Lib, with one child reading the words and asking the other to supply the part of speech or number. Once the blanks are filled in, the partners can work together to solve the resulting math problem.

4. Partners then trade places to complete the remaining problems. As a followup, let students create new Mad Lib-like math problems to share with the class.

Try This Too! Puddle Questions

Introduce your students to some of the open-ended problems from *Puddle Questions: Assessing Mathematical Thinking* by Joan Westley (Creative Publications, 1994). For example, a good question to ask is "How would you measure a puddle?" Have students write down their responses. Try this at the beginning of the year and then again at the end after you have worked on measurement and problem solving. These make good math portfolio pieces.

The Jelly Bean Contest
By Kathy Darling

Drawings by Buck Brown

The Jelly Bean Contest

by Kathy Darling (Garrard, 1972)

A group of boys wants to win a contest sponsored by the local candy store. They can win a football if they guess how many jelly beans are in a jar. The group comes up with a strategy and has Oscar, the smartest in math, make a guess. He's way off, so the youngest in the group suggests getting a jar similar to the one in the store. The older boys fill the jar with rocks of various sizes and try another guess. Wrong again. They try other estimation strategies, which bring them closer but not close enough to win. Finally, the youngest boy makes a guess based on the largest number he knows and wins.

Math Vocabulary

algorithm: a step-by-step method for computing

sample: a number of people, objects, or events chosen from a given population to represent the entire group

Sharing the Story

Either before or after reading this story, give students a copy of page 75, the jelly bean mosaic. Ask them at a glance to estimate the number of jelly beans in the mosaic and record it on the back of the paper. Discuss strategies for getting a closer estimate. Suggest the idea of counting a sample section. Demonstrate how to use a ruler and pencil to divide the picture into roughly even pieces. Ask what a next step might be (counting the jelly beans in a piece and then multiplying by the number of pieces.) Compare students' answers after the multiplication. How close are they?

NCTM STANDARDS

Problem Solving

Use problem solving to build mathematical knowledge.

- Apply various strategies to solve problems that arise in mathematics and other contexts.

Reasoning and Proof

Recognize reasoning and proof as fundamental aspects of mathematics.

- Investigate mathematical conjectures.

- Select and use various types of reasoning and methods of proof.

One Dollar Bill

The Jelly Bean Contest introduces a variety of estimation strategies. Explain to students that estimation is not just a guess, it is a "reasonable" guess based on reasoning and previous knowledge. Invite students to name things they can estimate—for example, speed, temperature, weight, and height, as well as how many of something. Practice those skills with this small-group activity.

1. Divide the class into groups of three or four. Give each student a copy of the letter on page 76, which is the story of the outlaw known as One Dollar Bill. He used to rob stagecoaches, but would only steal one-dollar bills.

2. Present an empty covered shoe box to the class and indicate that this was the size of Bill's box. Ask, "How much money could possibly be inside?" Give students paper, scissors, calculators, and rulers as tools to help them try to figure out and make a reasonable estimate of how much money could fit in the box. They may measure the outside of the box but not open it.

3. Have groups present their answers and thinking and have the class comment on the reasonableness of the work. At the end, give each participant a treat that you have pre-packed in the box.

Tip

Allow several sessions for completing this activity.

Try This Too! Thinking Stretcher

Discuss with students how estimation, reasoning, and proof are all related. Offer a problem for students to solve—for example, 167 - 79. Have students explain their thinking (most will use a conventional algorithm), then ask them to solve the same problem in a different way and explain their reasoning. Let students write a new problem, solve it, and write their explanation. Have them trade papers, solve each other's problems a different way, and discuss their reasoning. This activity stretches students' thinking and reinforces the practice of reasoning.

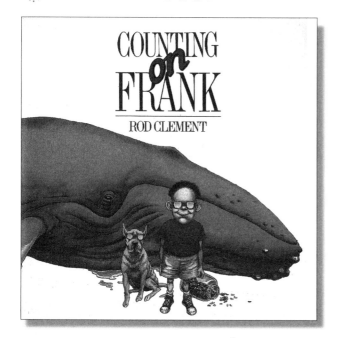

Counting on Frank

by Rod Clement (Gareth Stevens Publishing, 1991)

Frank is a dog that wears sunglasses and serves as a point of reference for some zany estimating and calculating done by his owner, a young boy. For example, the boy muses, "My dog, Frank, is pretty big and takes up a lot of space. I calculate that twenty-four Franks could fit into my bedroom. But sometimes there isn't even room for one." The boy estimates what would happen if his toaster were the size of the house, or if he knocked fifteen peas off his plate every night for eight years. In the end, all his estimation and calculation practice really pays off.

Sharing the Story

Before reading the story, display a sturdy shoe box or other small box. Place a marble alongside it. Have students estimate and write down how many marbles they think would fit in the box. Once students have their initial estimates, begin to fill the box with marbles, counting aloud one by one as you do. Stop when the box is half full. Invite students to revise their estimates at this point based on what they've observed. Continue counting and putting marbles in the box. When you are at about the $\frac{3}{4}$ mark, stop again and invite further revision of estimates. Finish filling the box and ask students to compare their estimates to the actual number of marbles in the box. Point out that the more information and experience students had about the marbles in the box, the more accurate their estimates became. Try this again using the same box, but with other objects such as unifix cubes, table-tennis balls, and tennis balls. Check estimates by filling the box and counting the actual objects.

Really Wild Classroom Estimation

Materials

- ☼ yardsticks
- ☼ tape measures
- ☼ calculators
- ☼ cardboard
- ☼ scissors
- ☼ tape

The boy in *Counting on Frank* made some pretty wild estimates and calculations, such as how many whales could fit in his house. You can have the same sort of fun with your class.

1. Have students use yardsticks and tape measures to measure the height, width, and length of their classroom (in feet).

2. Using these figures, have students calculate the volume of the room in square feet (height times width times length).

3. Cut and tape cardboard to create a square-foot box. Each edge should measure one foot.

4. Now comes the fun! Fill the box with anything and count how much of the item is inside. Multiply that number by the number of square feet in the room (which you calculated earlier), and you can figure things like about how many marbles, tennis balls, yo-yos, or gumballs it would take to fill your room!

Try This Too! Volume vs. Weight

Students at this age sometimes operate with the misconception that items of equal volume have equal weight—that a jar of honey weighs the same as a jar of cereal, as long as it's the same-size jar. It's fun to help students learn more about these ideas by filling various containers with different substances and letting students use simple balance scales to observe the difference themselves. For example, let students fill a plastic cup with split peas and place it on the balance, then fill an identical cup with popped popcorn and place it on the other side. Same volume—radically different weight! Good discussions can ensue about why.

Wacky Math Fill-Ins

1. Once there was a _____ who had
   (noun)

   _____ boxes of _____ .
   (three-digit number)   (plural noun)

   She/He gave her/his best friend, _____ ,
   (person in the class)

   _____ of the boxes. How many boxes did
   (two-digit number)

   she/he have left? _____

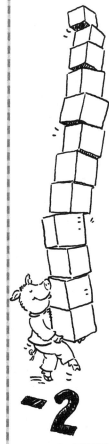

2. _____ loves _____
   (name of a teacher)   (adjective)

   _____ . She/He bought _____
   (plural noun)   (two-digit number)

   at a _____ and
   (place)

   _____ more at a _____ .
   (two-digit number)   (place)

   How many did she/he have all together? _____

3. Chief Super Spy _____
   (name of student)

   had _____ special _____ .
   (two-digit number)   (plural noun)

   She/He had to give them out evenly to her/his

   _____ fellow spies. How many should
   (one-digit number except 0 or 1)

   she/he give to each spy? _____

Meeting the Math Standards With Favorite Picture Books   Scholastic Professional Books

Jelly Bean Mosaic

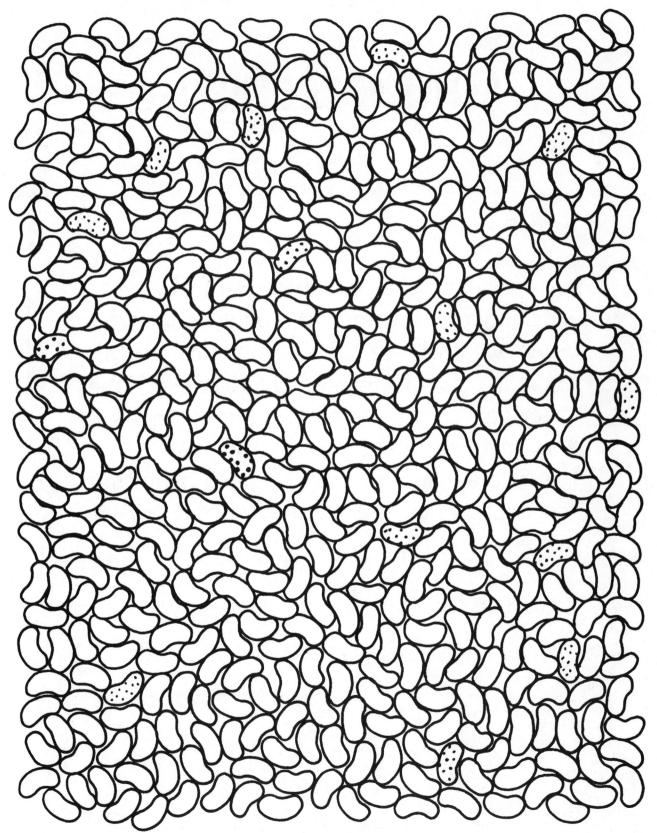

One Dollar Bill

OFFICE OF THE SHERIFF

Dear Students,

You have before you a box that I believe belonged to the notorious bank robber, One Dollar Bill. He was a strange one, Bill was. He stole only one-dollar bills. Does the box contain his last haul? It might. Then again, it might not. Try to reckon, or estimate, how much money could be in the box. Show your work and give your reasons. Then check it out.

Good luck pardners,

Sheriff Bat Matherston

Meeting the Math Standards With Favorite Picture Books   Scholastic Professional Books

More Books for Making Math Connections

In addition to the 25 titles featured in this book, try these suggestions for extending students' learning in the following areas of mathematics: number and operations; patterns and algebra; geometry and spatial sense; measurement; data analysis and probability; and reasoning, proof, and problem-solving.

NUMBER

Can You Count to a Googol?
by Robert Wells (Albert Whitman, 2000)
The author uses lots of multiplication and cartoon illustrations to bring readers along through millions, billions, trillions, and the googol!

Fraction Action
by Loreen Leedy (Holiday House, 1994)
Five fun stories tell about characters who use fractions in their everyday lives.

Fraction Fun
by David Adler (Holiday House, 1996)
This instructional book features some good experiments and activities with simple fractions ($\frac{1}{2}, \frac{1}{3}, \frac{1}{4}, \frac{1}{8}$).

The History of Counting
by Denise Schmandt-Besserat (Morrow, 1999)
This colorful book looks at counting systems throughout history and around the world.

How Much, How Many, How Far, How Heavy, How Long, How Tall Is 1,000?
by Helen Noland (Kids Can Press, 1995)
Explores 1,000 in terms of weight, length, number, and height, with fun illustrations and examples from real life.

The King's Commissioners
by Aileen Friedman (Scholastic, 1995)
The king counts his many commissioners one by one but then gets advice to try skip-counting.

A Million Fish More or Less
by Patricia McKissack (Dragonfly, 1996)
Brilliant, colorful illustrations depict a Louisiana Bayou tale good for introducing ideas about number and counting at higher levels.

On Beyond a Million: An Amazing Math Journey
by David M. Schwartz (Doubleday/Random House, 1999)
This book provides many fun facts about large numbers, animals, the human body . . . even Tootsie Rolls.

OPERATIONS

Amanda Bean's Amazing Dream: A Mathematical Story
by Cindy Neuschwander (Scholastic, 1998)
Amanda is not convinced multiplication will be much good until she has an amazing dream.

Anno's Mysterious Multiplying Jar
by Masaichiro and Mitsumasa Anno
(Philomel, 1983)
Extend multiplication thinking in complex ways with a story about a mysterious jar.

The Great Divide
by Dayle Ann Dodds
(Candlewick Press, 1999)
A group in a cross-country race is continually divided in half as the race narrows down to the one winner. You might be surprised who it is!

Mission Addition
by Loreen Leedy (Holiday House, 1997)
Miss Prime and her class make up word problems, add large numbers, and check their work. Bright illustrations and a playful sense of humor add to this picture book's appeal.

Sea Squares
by Joy Hulme (Hyperion, 1991)
"Four seals with four flippers each makes sixteen slippery feet." Rhyming examples of multiples from the ocean fill the pages of this lovely book.

Shark Swimathon
by Stuart Murphy (HarperCollins, 2000)
Follow along on a fun excursion as a shark swim team practices both swimming and subtraction.

Ten Sly Piranhas
by William Wise (Dial, 1993)
Join in on tongue-in-cheek rhyming text as piranhas get rid of each other one by one.

PATTERNS AND ALGEBRA

Anno's Magic Seeds
by Mitsumasa Anno (Paper Star, 1999)
A young boy plants enchanted seeds following a number pattern that becomes fairly complex as he grows older, has a family, and continues planting and harvesting.

Ben Franklin and the Magic Squares
by Frank Murphy (Random House, 2001)
This book takes a look at Franklin's life as an inventor and provides an explanation of how his magic square number patterns work.

Eight Hands Round: A Patchwork Alphabet
by Ann Whitford Paul
(HarperCollins, 1991)
This book explores traditional patterns of quilting with great illustrations and stories about each pattern.

A Grain of Rice
by Helena Clare Pittman (Hastings House, 1986)
This is another version of *The King's Chessboard* doubling idea, with this one taking place in China.

Insides, Outsides, Loops, and Lines
by Herbert Kohl (Freeman, 1995)
Exploring patterns other than number, Kohl moves from simple to complex, using examples such as maps and Mobius strips.

Science in Our World
(Grolier, 1993)
This helpful reference book explores patterns and shapes as the basis of many designs in the world around us.

Meeting the Math Standards With Favorite Picture Books   Scholastic Professional Books

GEOMETRY AND SPATIAL SENSE

The Amazing Book of Shapes
by Lydia Sharman (Dorling Kindersley, 1994)
Colorful photo illustrations depict real-life examples of shapes around us. Includes simple project ideas kids will like and can do.

Arrow to the Sun: A Pueblo Indian Tale
by Gerald McDermott (Viking, 1974)
This Native-American Sun legend features vibrant, graphic, geometric-based illustrations. Kids can enjoy this story and have a good time finding all the shapes embedded in the illustrations.

Pigs on the Ball: Fun With Math and Sports
by Amy Axelrod (Simon & Schuster, 1998)
The Pig family goes to a miniature golf course and encounters lots of fun and geometry.

Round Buildings, Square Buildings, Buildings That Wiggle Like a Fish
by Philip Isaacson (Knopf, 1988)
Beautiful color photo examples of architecture around the world with a focus on shapes and patterns of pathways, doorways, walls, and other building elements. Great for real-life examples of geometry around us.

MEASUREMENT

If You Hopped Like a Frog
by David M. Schwartz (Scholastic, 1999)
Great cartoon-style examples help students explore ratio and proportion through measurement. Mathematical discussions and explanations are included for both teacher and student.

Jim and the Beanstalk
by Raymond Briggs (Paper Star, 1997)
This updated, humorous version of the classic story of Jack features a good deal of measurement and proportion.

Pigs in the Pantry: Fun With Math and Cooking
by Amy Axelrod (Simon & Schuster, 1997)
Inadequate attention to careful measurement while cooking leads Mr. Pig and the piglets to some bad results. This simple story makes a good connection to math in the kitchen.

Ultimate Kids' Money Book
by Neale S. Godfrey (Simon & Schuster, 1998)
This thorough, lively resource covers everything about money, including credit cards, checks, banks, budgets, and coins.

What's Faster Than a Speeding Cheetah?
by Robert Wells (Albert Whitman, 1997)
The speeds of animals, machines, people, and even meteorites are compared in this very interesting and engaging picture book—great for beginning a discussion on how speed is measured.

DATA AND PROBABILITY

Do You Wanna Bet?: Your Chance to Find Out About Probability

by Jean Cushman (Clarion Books, 1991)

This book features problems in story contexts that focus on how data can inform predictions. It offers many good examples of practical applications of probability and data analysis.

Jumanji

by Chris Van Allsburg (Houghton Mifflin, 1981)

This Caldecott winner is a classic. Incredible pencil illustrations help tell the tale of a mysterious board game. Probability, chance, and a roll of the dice can have dire consequences in this book.

Let's Investigate Statistics

by Marion Smoothey (Marshall Cavendish, 1993)

Textbook-style explanations and good definitions help explain data analysis and representation.

Lemonade for Sale

by Stuart Murphy (HarperCollins, 1998)

Three children and their parrot have a lemonade stand and keep track of their sales data with bar graphs. This basic introduction to organizing and graphing data will inspire lots of applications.

Pigs at Odds: Fun With Math and Games

by Amy Axelrod (Simon & Schuster, 2000)

The Pig family enjoys games of chance at the country fair, making this book a good springboard for talking about probability.

REASONING, PROOF, AND PROBLEM SOLVING

Betcha!

by Stuart Murphy (HarperCollins, 1997)

Two boys use estimation strategies as they try to win a contest by guessing the correct number of jelly beans in a jar.

Easy Math Puzzles

by David Adler (Holiday House, 1997)

Clever puzzles feature a combination of math and language thinking, great for using in a "problem of the day" format.

The Eleventh Hour: A Curious Mystery

by Graeme Base (Abrams, 1993)

Detailed illustrations and a mystery in verse compel readers to use critical thinking and problem-solving skills.

The I Hate Mathematics! Book

by Marilyn Burns (Little, Brown, 1975)

Designed to excite the reluctant mathematician, this engaging resource features clever mental math, magic tricks, geometry, measurement, and number patterns. Look for *Math for Smarty Pants* by the same author, too.

Mental Math Challenges

by Michael Lobosco (Sterling, 1999)

Lots of interesting and challenging projects incorporate geometry, measurement, games, and tricks. Photos help readers follow directions.

Meeting the Math Standards With Favorite Picture Books   Scholastic Professional Books